MEN AT AR

Echoes of War

MEN AT ARNHEM

GEOFFREY POWELL

BUCHAN & ENRIGHT, PUBLISHERS
LONDON

First published, under the name 'Tom Angus', in Great Britain in 1976 by
Leo Cooper Ltd
This edition (revised) published in 1986 by
Buchan & Enright, Publishers, Ltd
53 Fleet Street, London EC4Y 1BE

British Library Cataloguing in Publication Data

Powell, Geoffrey
Men at Arnhem.—(Echoes of war)
1. Great Britain. *Army*—Parachute troops
2. World War, 1939–1945—Personal narratives,
British   3. Arnhem (Netherlands), Battle of,
1944
I. Title   II. Series
940.54'21'0924   D763.N4
ISBN 0–907675–71–9

Printed in Great Britain by
Redwood Burn Limited, Trowbridge, Wiltshire and
bound by Pegasus Bookbinding, Melksham, Wiltshire
Cover printed by The Furnival Press, London

CONTENTS

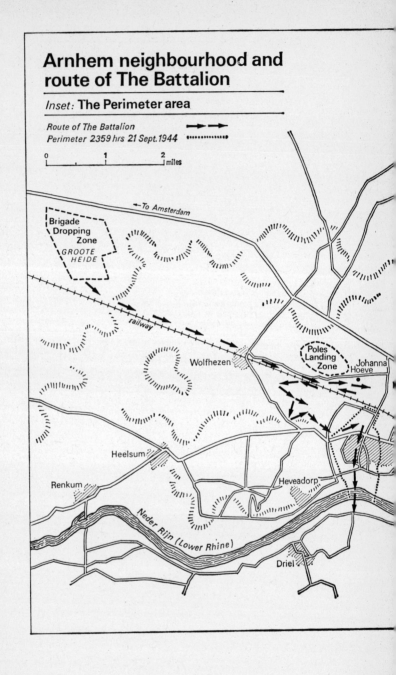

Arnhem neighbourhood and route of The Battalion

Inset: **The Perimeter area**

Route of The Battalion
Perimeter 2359 hrs 21 Sept. 1944 ••••••••••••

0   1   2 ┐ miles

←To Amsterdam

Brigade
Dropping
Zone
GROOTE
HEIDE

railway

Wolfhezen

Poles
Landing
Zone

Johanna
Hoeve

Heelsum

Renkum

Heveadorp

Neder Rijn (Lower Rhine)

Driel

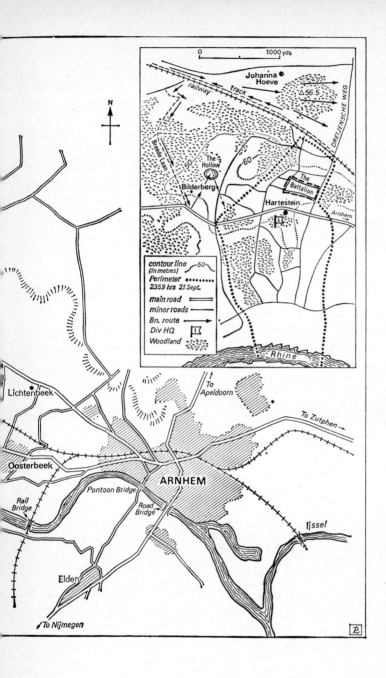

0   1000 yds

Johanna Hoeve

△56.5

railway   track

DREIJENSCHE WEG

Bredde Laan

50   The Hollow   60

Bilderberg

The Battalion

Hartestein

Arnhem

contour line (in metres) ···50···
Perimeter 2359 hrs 21 Sept. ••••••
main road
minor roads
Bn. route →
Div HQ
Woodland

Rhine

N

Lichtenbeek

To Apeldoorn

To Zutphen →

Oosterbeek

ARNHEM

Pontoon Bridge

Rail Bridge

Road Bridge

Ijssel

Elden

To Nijmegen

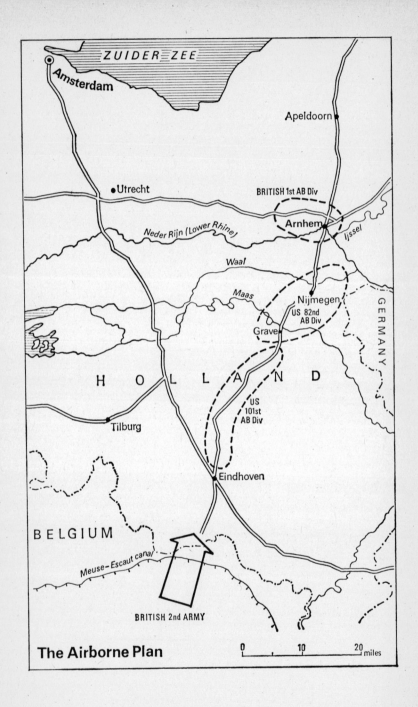

ZUIDER ZEE

Amsterdam

Apeldoorn

Utrecht

BRITISH 1st AB Div

Neder Rijn (Lower Rhine)

Arnhem

Ijssel

Waal

Maas

Nijmegen

US 82nd
AB Div

Grave

GERMANY

H O L L A N D

US
101st
AB Div

Tilburg

Eindhoven

BELGIUM

Meuse–Escaut canal

BRITISH 2nd ARMY

The Airborne Plan

0   10   20 miles

THE BATTALION

Its organisation when it went into action, showing the appointments held by those officers and men mentioned in chapters 1-4

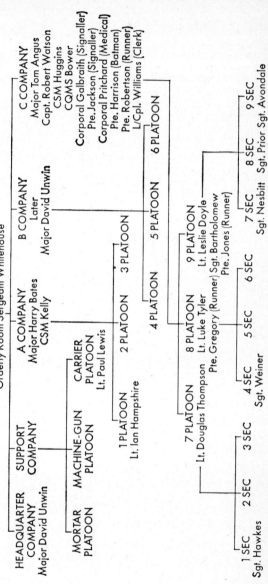

HEADQUARTERS

The Colonel, The Adjutant, The Doctor
Captain Jimmy Gray (Regimental Signal Officer)
Captain John Simmonds (Gunner F.O.O. attached)
Lieutenant and Quartermaster Hugh Elkins
The RSM
Orderly Room Sergeant Whitehouse

HEADQUARTER COMPANY
Major David Unwin

SUPPORT COMPANY

A COMPANY
Major Harry Bates
CSM Kelly

B COMPANY
Later
Major David Unwin

C COMPANY
Major Tom Angus
Capt. Robert Watson
CSM Huggins
CQMS Bower
Corporal Galbraith (Signaller)
Pte. Jackson (Signaller)
Corporal Pritchard (Medical)
Pte. Harrison (Batman)
Pte. Robertson (Runner)
L/Cpl. Williams (Clerk)

MORTAR PLATOON

MACHINE-GUN PLATOON

CARRIER PLATOON
Lt. Paul Lewis

1 PLATOON
Lt. Ian Hampshire

2 PLATOON

3 PLATOON

4 PLATOON

5 PLATOON

6 PLATOON

7 PLATOON
Lt. Douglas Thompson

8 PLATOON
Lt. Luke Tyler
Pte. Gregory (Runner)

9 PLATOON
Lt. Leslie Doyle
Sgt. Bartholomew
Pte. Jones (Runner)

1 SEC
Sgt. Hawkes

2 SEC

3 SEC

4 SEC
Sgt. Weiner

5 SEC

6 SEC

7 SEC
Sgt. Nesbitt

8 SEC

9 SEC
Sgt. Prior Sgt. Avondale

CHAPTER ONE

ARRIVAL

THE black cloud of smoke exploded silently outside the open door of the Dakota, obscuring for the moment my view of the geometrical Dutch landscape, deserted but for a few forlorn cows.

As soon as the sea had appeared below us, I started to think about the flak, and I knew that everyone else in the aircraft must be worrying as well. When we crossed the East Anglian coastline, that slight wave of movement had flickered down the aircraft, as men checked their watches, calculating the time it would take to fly over the sea and come within range of the now alerted German anti-aircraft guns. Below us, the air-sea rescue launches of the RAF, dotting the water at precise intervals, were pleasantly comforting.

The narrow band of beach which was the coast of Holland had aroused us once again. As the flooded fields flashed into view, Private Harrison had leaned across to point out the guns on the ground shooting up at the massed ranks of our aircraft. At the sound of my batman's voice, which had been silent for the past hour, the men near to the open doorway had craned forward to see what they could, while the rest, anxious for the first indications of the enemy, had twisted their necks to peer through the small windows at their backs.

At first I could see nothing, and I was stupidly aggravated

that everyone but myself could spot the gun-flashes. Then came that cloud of smoke, producing an odd sense of satisfaction, a fatuous reaction which immediately shamed me. This was the behaviour of a small boy. For all that, it was satisfying not to feel scared by it: perhaps it was because the experience was not only novel, but in some way impersonal. Looking down the dark tunnel of the aircraft at the double line of soldiers, it was a relief to see that all traces of nervousness had disappeared.

We had all been waiting a long time for this. The morning before, I had been clearing up the paperwork, signing a few returns and checking the company accounts, seated at the trestle table which served as a desk in the bare company office, a groom's bedroom over the red-brick stable block of a Leicestershire hunting-box. In the loose-boxes below, my hundred or so men lived in the space previously occupied by a quarter the number of hunters.

For an hour I had been waiting for the sound. Now it came, a faint drone in the distance which quickly swelled into a great throbbing roar. I dived for the single small window, but the CQMS, Colour-Sergeant Bower, who had that moment entered the room with a couple of missing receipts in his hand, reached it first and threw up the sash. Peering up, we could just see above the roof-tops, half visible through the clouds, column after column of Dakota aircraft, stout and solid, disappearing overhead towards the east. So it had happened after all. This time we really were going. It was the first lift. Even Bower, that imperturbable Scot, was leaping up and down in his excitement.

Together the two of us turned and raced for the door, all but colliding on the landing with Huggins, the CSM, who, halting in his tracks as I passed, sprang to attention before following us down the stairs two at a time. Lance-Corporal Williams, the young company clerk, brought up the rear. As the four of us reached the stable-yard, the hundred men of 'C' Company were pouring out of the looseboxes, half-dressed, hardly able to believe that it could be happening. They watched in silence, gazing up towards the waves of transport aircraft throbbing overhead.

During the past three years, such aircraft had become a part of our lives: transport squadrons operating in ones and twos in the Middle East; large fleets collected for the invasion of Sicily and the long series of training exercises which had filled the waiting months prior to D-Day; and more of them still as the night bombers gathered in the evening light before they turned towards the cities of Germany. But this was something even bigger, and even this was no more than a part of the vast American and British airborne armada brought together to fly the three divisions, one British and two American, into Holland. We had come a long way since the days in Delhi when we first learned to jump from the superannuated squadron of Vickers Valentia biplanes, string-bags out of a First World War movie.

Now only two things could stop us leaving on the second lift tomorrow morning – bad weather or such heavy losses to the aircraft flying overhead that not enough would return for the next flight. Ever since D-Day we had been waiting for this. No, that was wrong! Ever since the Battalion was formed in 1941. We had, of course, landed from the sea at Taranto, and then chased the retreating Germans up the heel of Italy, but that had amounted to little more than the chance to learn what it was like to be shot at. In the whole Brigade, less than a hundred men had been killed or wounded. For three years or so, we had done little more than play at being soldiers, the weeks and months filled by an endless succession of training exercises.

13

We were hard and well-led, and we knew our job, even though we had seen so little of the real thing. In fact, we were now, if anything, overtrained. Many of the soldiers were prewar regulars who had volunteered for parachuting to escape the tedium of scorching Indian cantonments, where they seemed fated to rot for the rest of the war. We always seemed to be left out. The other British airborne division, the 6th, had fought hard in the D-Day landings and afterwards in Normandy. In our own division, we envied the 1st Parachute Brigade, whose battles in Tunisia and Sicily had established the fame of the red beret and caught the eye of the British public. For years now we had sat on our arses, living in what passed for comfort in wartime, while the infantry were slaughtered in Burma, Africa, Italy and France. How ironic it was! Most of us had left one of those infantry battalions to try to find a quicker way to the fighting, only to be trapped in a never-ending round of training exercises.

Since D-Day we had prepared for sixteen different parachute operations. Some had been cancelled before the men had even been briefed, others as they were waiting for trucks to take them to the airfield. Some came to nothing because the forces on the ground moved too slowly, others because they had swept forward too successfully. Some were straightforward military operations, others exotic, like the one in which we were to help raise the French Maquis. Some might have succeeded; others would have been suicidal. It was understandable that nerves had frayed and discipline been upset during the summer. More and more men had drifted away, absent without leave, to return when boredom set in or consciences started to bite. Fights outside pubs with GIs from nearby American units had become a regular Saturday night fixture in the Midland cities and market towns. After the hysteria of the capture of Paris, the British and American

14

armies were still sweeping on towards the German frontier, virtually unopposed. The war could well be over before we got into it. 'The Stillborn Division', we had started to call ourselves, to be kept for use in the victory parade, nice and tidy in our smart, red berets.

There was nothing more to do for the rest of the day. The briefings were over, and now everyone should know in exact detail everything which had to be done from the moment of landing. I had pored over the maps and aerial photographs for so many hours that I needed only to close my eyes to visualize the sandy countryside west of Arnhem where we would land. Arnhem! Knowing so much now about the town, it seemed odd that I had hardly heard of the place until a few days ago.

Everyone's kit had been checked, double-checked and packed. Not only the weapons, but every round of ammunition had been cleaned and inspected with meticulous care: always in our minds was the danger of jamming Stens and Bren guns. The escape kits of miniature saws, compasses and silk maps had been sewn into the linings of clothes, and the syringes of morphia had been issued. Personal belongings had been packed and stored. By now it was so much a matter of routine that the various chores had been done automatically.

Now I needed to get through the afternoon and evening. Like everyone else, I was not allowed outside the billets except to walk the few hundred yards up the road to the mess. The men must be left alone. It was important not to fuss or over-organize them. The preparations had all been made.

Back in the office, I turned once again to the operation order lying on the desk, the maps and the photographs, pondering once more over the details, anxious that no point might have been missed. The plan seemed simple and straightforward, as all sound military plans should be, but as I worked through it, the same two doubts once again nagged. Why did there have to be two lifts? Surely the allocation of aircraft between the three divisions could have been so arranged that the whole of the division was dropped on Arnhem together? The other worry was the distance between the dropping zone west of Arnhem and the low hills to the north of the city which we were to hold after the 1st Brigade had seized the bridges over the Rhine. It was at least eight miles, and the men would be carrying very heavy loads. Had too much attention been paid to the flak which was supposed to ring Arnhem, and too little to the opposition on the ground which the Boche might produce during the landings and the march into the city. I had discussed these doubts with no one, not even with David Unwin, with whom I could talk about anything. In the present atmosphere of optimism and relief, they were thoughts which it would be unfair to share.

Sweeping up the papers, I locked them in the safe. It was quite pointless to worry. I knew what had to be done in my own small corner of the battlefield and nothing else mattered. The divisional plan was no concern of mine. It was nearly time for lunch; I picked up my beret and belt and started down the stairs.

At the gate, Private Gregory, who was on sentry duty, saluted, grinning as he did so. I stopped for a word. Isolated as he had been for the past hour by the gate, Gregory was anxious for a chat. The look of happy satisfaction on his weatherbeaten face was good to see. An old regular, he had joined the Battalion on the day it was formed. When he arrived back in England the previous Christmas, he had gone on leave to his home in Middlesbrough to learn that his young brother, whom he had not seen for nine years, had just been reported missing in Burma. Except for hearing a few bullets fired by Wazir tribesmen, Gregory had never been in action. The fact rankled with him even more than most, so much so that it had become an obsession.

Standing together by the ornate double-gate, the two of us agreed that there was little to worry about. The chances of that lot up there being brought back were slim indeed, and by tomorrow we would all be over in Holland.

Everyone was in the mess, including a couple of gunner captains, Forward Observation Officers, who would drop as part of the Battalion. There was also a strange French subaltern, his rôle both unexplained and inexplicable, who was to accompany us.

Unnoticed for the moment, I stood near the door and watched them. For the past three years, for the greater part of the war in fact, I had played and worked with at least half of the people in the room. Life before 1939 was a remote memory, unreal and unimportant. Living cheek by jowl, I felt that I understood most of them better than the members of my own family. They were my life now, they and the six hundred or so soldiers, many of whom I knew just as well. We were a closed community, wary of outsiders, drawing our strength from one another.

Harry Bates, who commanded 'A' Company, beckoned to me. I waited on the edge of their chatter, listening to the stereotyped generalizations, peculiar to the circumstances. I had heard it all before. As if to apologize for their self-confidence, they were pretending to be scared by the sudden arrival of reality, competing together in their lies, the older ones regretting their failure to secure safe billets in such comfortable refuges as the War Office.

17

Five minutes of this was enough. Across the room I caught David Unwin's eye, and the two of us carried our drinks to a corner where no one was likely to intrude. As the two senior company commanders, both a year short of thirty, we were the oldest officers in the Battalion, except for the Colonel.

We laughed together about McGee and Inglis, two absentees from David's Headquarter Company, who had that morning appeared out of the blue and walked into the CSM's office. I knew them nearly as well as David did, two Scots with conduct sheets nearly a yard long. By some strange bush-telegraph, they must have heard that something was happening and had returned to give themselves up, hoping to be allowed to rejoin their platoons and take their punishment afterwards. How well the two men had judged the outcome! Like us all, they knew the Colonel's foibles. After a tongue-lashing, they had been awarded twenty-eight days field punishment, with instructions that they be released from arrest to join their platoons. Room for them had been found in a plane, and now David's CQMS was kitting them up instead of relaxing in the Sergeants' Mess. David made no effort to hide his pleasure at their return. Nevertheless, it was worrying how the news had reached them.

And so the warm September afternoon drifted aimlessly by. At 6 o'clock we gathered again to hear the BBC news, disappointing in the poverty of its detail.

My wife and I had found a minute flat in the town – we had been married just three months before – but since the Battalion had been confined to billets three nights ago, I had shared Ian Hampshire's room, the only spare corner in the overcrowded building.

Hampshire was a tall, gangling subaltern in 'A' Company,

barely twenty years old, who had joined the Battalion just before D-Day. Faced with a 3 am start, we had both gone to bed early, but sleep eluded us. We chatted, or rather Hampshire did, talking in the manner of the young about himself, his OCTU, his school, his platoon and his family. There was no need to do more than insert a word from time to time to keep the flow running. By talking himself to sleep in this way, Hampshire could forget the problems of the next day. It seemed absurd that the previous summer this boy had been playing for his school XI, while tomorrow he would be in charge of thirty men, nearly all of them older than him. It was an odd system, but it seemed to work well. Almost in mid-sentence the boy fell asleep.

Someone was shaking my arm. Forcing my eyes open, I blinked at the glare from the unshaded light hanging in the middle of the room. The sight of CSM Huggins, fully dressed and immaculate as ever, made my heart sink. Surely it could not be another cancellation? But it was only a two-hour delay. It was midnight now, so reveille could be changed to 0500 hours. Five hours more sleep. Was there anything worse than leaving a warm bed at 3 o'clock with a jump ahead and no prospect of seeing it again for several days to come? Then I remembered that this was not another training drop, and that there were indeed worse things.

I told Huggins to wake the sergeants and officers and give them the news. CQMS Bower, who shared a room with Huggins, would know already. The others could just be left to sleep on for another couple of hours.

Because of the delay the convoy of trucks started for the airfield not in the quiet darkness of the early morning, but just as the town was stirring. An earlier start might have dampened the men's exhilaration, but I doubted it. The noise of a dozen songs poured out of the back of the trucks. They were deliberately trying to wake the town so that they could say good-bye to the people who had treated us so well during the past six months. They wanted to bring everyone out into the streets to see us go.

The long lines of pot-bellied Dakotas drawn up on the runway brought home once again the immense scope of it all. At more than twenty other airfields across the country trucks were disgorging their loads of men and vehicles by the side of waiting aircraft and gliders. The same thing had happened yesterday, and it would happen again tomorrow if all went well. I had read about the preparations for D-Day, but now I could see for myself the size of the American and British war effort. And then there were the Russians too. After the years of struggle, it was nearly over. The Germans were all but beaten. I knew, as we all did, that to win this battle would prevent another winter of war.

Now came the familiar toil of struggling into jumping kit. Over my battle-dress and airborne smock, I was already wearing full equipment: the haversack containing maps, torch and other odds and ends; respirator, water-bottle and compass; pistol holster and ammunition case; and on my chest the two pouches crammed with Sten magazines and hand grenades. Across my stomach I then tied my small pack, solid with two days' concentrated rations, mess tin, spare socks, washing kit, pullover, a tin mug, all topped with a Hawkins anti-tank grenade. Slung around my neck were binoculars, while a large shell dressing, a morphia syringe and red beret were tucked into my smock pockets. Next I wrapped myself in a denim jumping jacket to hold the bits and pieces in place and prevent the parachute cords snagging on the many protuberances. Over everything went

20

a Mae West life-jacket, with a camouflage net scarfed around my neck and the parachutist's steel helmet, covered with a scrim-decorated net, on my head. On to my right leg I then tied a large bag, into which was packed a Sten gun, together with an oblong-shaped walkie-talkie radio, and a small entrenching tool; a quick release catch allowed this bag to be lowered in mid-air so that it would dangle below on a thin cord and hit the ground before I did. Next Private Harrison helped me into my parachute, and I did the same for him, after which we both tested each other's quick release boxes to make certain that they were working properly.

We were loaded like pack donkeys – one of the drawbacks of being taken into battle by air with so few vehicles available to carry kit. If we were to eat, drink, dig and fight with some hope of success against the heavily equipped German troops who were waiting for us, we would need everything we were carrying. As it was, we had enough food and ammunition for only a day or two. More should arrive in the supply drops, but upon this we could not depend.

After much thought, I had decided to take two luxuries, a red beret and an *Oxford Book of English Verse*. More often than not, airborne troops found themselves fighting on with the infantry for weeks or even months after they had linked up with the ground forces. If this were to happen to us, I would want to spare my head from the burden of its tin hat, and I was always unhappy without a book within reach.

During my inspection, I checked with care that everyone had emptied his pockets of every scrap of paper, not only operational instructions and notes, but even personal letters which might reveal some detail to the enemy such as the name of our unit. Afterwards CSM Huggins inspected me in the same way, hitting once again the quick release box of my parachute and going through the contents of my pockets.

Then visitors started to arrive. First it was the tea wagon,

21

manned by the WVS, but before I could swallow more than a mouthful, an RAF jeep tore up to our aircraft. Out of it stepped the Colonel, dapper as ever and still unencumbered by his operational kit. My heart lifted, as it often did, at the sight of this tall, austere man, only three years older than myself, so modest in his wisdom and knowledge. He was a regular soldier of the type so often produced by the Guards, professionally skilled and enthusiastic, with an independence of mind based on self-confidence and private means. In his eighteen months with the Battalion, the Colonel had transformed it into his personal instrument. Although he worked the men hard, and held them in check with a discipline harsh but fair, he failed to hide a kindly nature under a rather arid exterior. Not all his soldiers liked him, but there were few, if any, who did not respect him.

Not for the first time I reflected on our good fortune at being led into battle by a man like the Colonel.

Hoisting his long legs over the side of the jeep, the Colonel motioned to CSM Huggins to tell the men to sit down again. They had been struggling under their ungainly loads, hoisting themselves to their feet like recumbent cattle disturbed on a summer afternoon, but they now collapsed again sprawling on the grass. The Colonel wasted no time on preliminaries. His news was bad. Due to fog and low clouds on the airfields in the South of England, the take-off was to be delayed by a further couple of hours. Food, he told us, would be brought round soon, but in the meantime we should remove our parachutes and try to relax.

Was this the first stage in yet another cancelled operation? The unspoken dismay was obvious and the Colonel produced a smile of reassurance. We had no need to worry. There was no doubt at all that we would be going. The other two brigades were already fighting over there. Wishing us good luck, he reminded us that we would next meet in

Holland and was away, back in his jeep, off towards the next aircraft in the line.

We took off our parachutes and tried to relax. Luckily the next two hours passed quickly. We were used to waiting; so much of soldiering involved hanging about. And to help fill the time, there were more visitors. Trucks came with the promised meal, and later there was more tea. With it were the daily papers, splashing yesterday's drop in black headlines, but giving nothing away. Finally, just as we were once again heaving ourselves into our parachutes, the press photographers arrived. This they all loved. Despite their protests of bored cynicism, luridly expressed, they lined up in front of the cameras with alacrity, some faces decked with the coy, forced smiles of a party on Blackpool Pier, others as stolid as company footballers posing for a group photograph. The journalists must have been disappointed: there was nothing here to suggest rugged hard-bitten Red Devils.

The engines burst into a controlled roar as the American pilot tested each in turn. The familiar quiver of unease which always gripped me when I heard the noise returned. Only a cancellation in mid-flight would now avoid my having to throw myself through that door. Today's jump was no different from any other. This was the thirtieth, but the anticipation was still as unpleasant as ever. It was not the fear of injury, although on two different occasions I had broken a leg and knocked myself three parts silly. Neither was it dislike of hanging in mid-air; in fact the drift down towards the ground after the parachute had opened was an experience unique in its blend of aesthetic delight and physical satisfaction. The distaste must lie in the unnatural act of throwing oneself through that door into space. It would never become routine, and I knew that most men in the

23

Battalion felt the same, whatever their overt attitudes might be, some braggart, but more often exaggerated repulsion.

Nevertheless, I was glad that I was not in a glider. I had never set foot inside one, and never wanted to, despite an appetite avid for new experience. To lumber clumsily earthwards in such a flimsy ply-wood box had always seemed not only frightening but also lacking in the compensating pleasures to be found in parachuting. To be crushed against a tree as the object crumpled into matchwood was an unpleasant prospect and a not infrequent occurrence.

After tugging and pushing each others' unwieldy carcasses through the door of the aircraft, we were now sitting in the bucket seats which ran along each side of the fuselage. With the discomfort of sharp bits of equipment cutting into nearly every part of my body, I wondered how I would endure the next four long hours. But, as usual, this was soon forgotten, my attention gripped by what seemed to be a solid traffic jam of Dakotas three abreast on the runway as far as I could see in both directions.

In turn the Dakotas took off, circling above the airfield as they picked up formation. Everyone peered through the small windows behind, searching for familiar landmarks. I could see through the open door the endless stream of planes fading away into the distance. It was yesterday over again.

Now it was much the same as any training drop. Men showed their disquiet in a variety of ways. Some wrapped a blanket about themselves and immediately fell asleep, using oblivion to avoid their thoughts. Some smoked; one or two read. I looked at the brown-paper bag beside each seat and prayed that the pills which we had taken before the flight were potent. Even more than usual, I dreaded today the thought of a planeload of air-sick men. It was a horror experienced more than once in the past. I stole a glance towards Corporal Galbraith who was sitting a few places to my right. As usual he was staring at his bag, waiting for the inevitable. But today it was calm enough even for Galbraith. Copious amounts of food had been put aboard, but no one seemed hungry. Some even spurned the tea as being too sweet, a near unique complaint.

The black cloud vanished as quickly as it had arrived, left behind by the rushing plane. The anxiety had gone. The effect of coming under fire had been to steady everyone's nerves. Glancing up above the massed ranks of the Dakotas, I was delighted to see the shapes of allied fighters weaving in and out of the scattered clouds. So vast an airborne operation could not have been mounted if the Germans had been capable of putting a strong force of fighters into the sky. Nevertheless, they might always produce a few from somewhere or other. Any which then managed to elude the Allied fighter force were likely to prove much more frightening than mere flak.

Suddenly the flak was real. As I looked back down the line, the plane just behind seemed to lurch to one side, a bright red spot on its port wing glowing in the sunshine before it spread in a stream of flame towards the fuselage. Then the nose of the plane dipped, and it disappeared from view. No parachutes appeared. I knew that it carried men from the Battalion, and tried to stop speculating who was inside it.

The shout of 'twenty minutes to go' from the pilot's cabin cleared my mind. Immediately everyone was busy fiddling with equipment, tightening this and loosening that, passing cigarettes around for a final drag.

I had just started to think again about the men in the plane behind, thrown forward in a jumbled heap against the

25

pilot's cabin while the flames from the burning engine roared towards them, when the navigator's cry of 'action stations' jerked me to life. I heaved myself clumsily to my feet, snap-hooking the static-line of my parachute to the steel cord overhead. No one ever performed this action casually, and today everyone was as careful as ever. Men checked, then glanced up to make certain, then had a third look. Even though they could see the despatcher walking towards them to make his final inspection, no one failed to make trebly sure that his parachute was in fact fastened to the aircraft.

The RAF despatcher was an old friend, the instructor who had taken our stick through its refresher course at the Parachute Training School at Ringway six months before. Only yesterday had I learned that twenty-four of these sergeant-instructors had been given leave from the never-ending Ringway sausage-machine to act as despatchers for the operation. All had volunteered to come, and some enlightened staff officer had granted their wish. It was good to see the old familiar faces. It was better with someone one knew!

I braced myself at the open door, the first man in the stick to jump, gripping the fuselage in case a sudden jerk flung me out too soon. Leaning forward, feeling the wind whip my face, poring over the details of the placid Dutch landscape below, I could now see one or two cyclists dotting the otherwise deserted countryside. The flicker of the red warning light near my face told me that there was one minute to go. A railway line flashed below. The pattern of woods was as familiar as the view of the stable yard from the office window; the air photographs and the briefing model of the ground had imprinted the shapes on my mind. The pilots were dead on target. More often than not in the old days we had been dropped astray, but these Yanks always learned from their mistakes.

I never saw the red light turn to green. Harrison's hand slapped my shoulder. I was out of the door. The slip-stream hit me, flicking me sideways, and I fell away, just catching a glimpse of Harrison in the air above me and the tail of the aircraft flashing out of sight. Then I was floating, suspended gently in mid-air, my parachute canopied high. Others, who had jumped from the planes in front, were already on the ground, struggling to rid themselves of their harness. Clouds of yellow smoke, released by the pathfinders of the Independent Company to mark the dropping zones, spread over the circles of collapsed, discarded parachutes which ringed the heathland below. I picked out the familiar landmarks, in particular the corner of the wood where 'C' Company was to collect.

I looked up at a sky choked with hundreds of swaying parachutes, most of them patterned in green and brown camouflage, but others in a galaxy of colours, red and orange, purple, blue and yellow, vivid against the scattered white clouds. Every moment more aircraft arrived to disgorge their cargoes into the crowded air. Then I noticed the humming. We were being shot at from the ground. There were Boche on the dropping-zone. Something was badly wrong. An opposed landing, with the enemy firing as we hung from our parachutes or tried to collect our weapons before we could gather into a cohesive force on the ground, was something new for us in the British airborne forces. It had happened to the Boche, slaughtered in their hundreds as they fell to the ground in Crete; never after that had they attempted to mount an airborne operation. But still, suspended in mid-air, the bullets seemed no more harmless than the flak had done when I first saw it coming up towards the plane.

I was thinking of what would await us on the ground as I pulled the release catch on the kit-bag tied to my leg, and started to lower the burden by its long cord so that it dangled free. A sharp pain burned the knuckles of my left hand. Blood was seeping from my fingers. A bullet must have hit me – grazed me, anyway. But now the heathland was rushing up. Raising my hands to the lift webs, I pulled, and then the ground hit me with an uncomfortable jar. A bad landing.

I lay in the sunken road, listening to the bullets cracking overhead, at the same time striking the quick-release box on my chest to rid myself of the parachute. But the leg-straps had somehow jammed around a piece of equipment. Lying on my back, kicking and cursing, the wind kept catching the canopy and dragging me across the ground, twenty yards or so at a time. What a jump! Not only was I wasting precious time, but this sort of thing was dangerous. At any moment I might hurt myself, or a Boche would catch me in the sights of his rifle.

Suddenly something parted to free me. Shaking away the web of harness and cord, I wrenched off the jumping jacket and started to unpack the kit-bag. It took no more than a minute to drape myself with its contents and snap a magazine on to the Sten. Then I started towards the company rendezvous, conscious again of the pain from my bloodied fingers and angry at the wasted time. However, I could use the hand; nothing was broken, and the gashes were not deep.

It was a long way across the Groote Heide to the company rendezvous at the edge of the wood. First out of the aircraft, I had landed on the southern edge of the vast expanse of fading purple heathland. The distance was about a mile, but the gently rolling slopes made it look even further. Now walking, now running, I felt the weight of weapons and equipment, fit though I was. Bullets still cracked overhead, and mortar bombs were exploding on the Arnhem side of the dropping zone. In places the heather was burning. Somewhere there was quite a battle, but I seemed to be clear of it for the time being. I passed men unpacking weapon containers, the coloured parachutes still attached. Others were moving in small parties towards their collecting points. Someone bumped past on one of those absurd little motor cycles. A couple of men were wheeling a two-wheeled trolley, full of 3-inch mortar bombs. It all seemed to be quite calm and orderly. The machine was working. Then I started to pick up some of my own men; soon I had a dozen or so behind me.

No one seemed to be getting hurt despite all the bullets flying around. Then I saw young Hampshire lying beside a collapsed parachute. The boy's right trouser leg had been cut away and a lance-corporal was tying a shell-dressing around his thigh. There could be no question of stopping. I could only commiserate as I passed by. The boy's response was cheerful, but he could not disguise the edge of pain in his voice. The NCO shouted after me that he had given the officer a shot of morphia and would find some stretcher-bearers.

Then at last, just ahead, was the edge of the wood, with Private Gregory standing by the side of the track, neat and calm as ever, waiting in just the right place to direct us towards the collecting point at the corner.

Twenty members of the company were already there, including Robert Watson, my second-in-command. From all directions, other men were approaching, some plodding, some breathless. Corporal Galbraith, headphones crammed down over his red beret, was talking into the radio, lying in the lee of a small bank, in which Private Jackson, the second signaller, was scratching a hole for the set with an entrenching tool.

Taking the headset from Galbraith so that I could report my arrival to Battalion Headquarters, I glanced around and was satisfied. Everyone was doing his appointed job without fuss. The long months of training had welded the men into a coherent unit. I felt confident.

A few yards from the radio set, a small green flag, emblazoned in yellow with a single crescent and star, had been planted under a tree. The year before, 'C' Company had jumped just outside Amman in a mock battle against the Emir of Transjordan's Frontier Force. It was more of a demonstration than a training exercise, and only a few minutes after we hit the ground, we had swarmed into the battlemented Beau Geste fort. The exotic Bedouin defenders, in flowing robes criss-crossed with bandoliers of ammunition and dagger-studded belts, had hauled the flag down from the battlements. Afterwards the apparently benign old ruler, who had watched the demonstration with a critical military eye, had presented the flag to the company. Since then it had been our totem. In camp or in billets, it had flown outside my office; on every march or exercise Robert Watson had carried it, tucked somewhere about him. Italy had given it the ultimate cachet – a bullet hole in one corner.

As I handed the head-set back to Galbraith, Corporal Pritchard appeared by my side. With a polite murmur of apology, more suited to the consulting-room than the battlefield, the medical orderly grasped my damaged hand and started to clean and bandage the fingers. I winced at the iodine sting, thinking not for the first time that I was glad not to be Pritchard, facing the battle without a weapon. As a deeply religious member of a lesser-known Nonconformist sect, Pritchard had chosen one of the more unpleasant options open to conscientious objectors.

A man with a blood-stained shell-dressing wrapped around his throat walked around the corner of the wood towards us just as Pritchard finished his work. Then came a couple of parties carrying stretchers, the occupant of one unconscious, the other with a cigarette between grey, tight lips. They were the first of a stream of wounded men from a variety of units, making their painful way towards the dressing station which had been set up in the wood behind us.

So far 'C' Company had been lucky. Only four men were missing and a fifth had turned up late, smiling cheerfully despite a bullet through his bandaged arm. Another four or five were limping and hopping about on strained or twisted ankles, expressions of disgust on their faces, victims of the gusty wind on the dropping-zone. All of them would have to be left behind. But then I thought again, calculating the figures once more. Perhaps we had not been so lucky after all. A tenth of the men who had emplaned that morning were already casualties.

It had sounded as if all the fighting had happened on the far side of the dropping-zone, in the Arnhem direction. Now the noise of the battle began to ebb; the enemy posts had probably been overrun. Neither news nor orders had arrived from Battalion HQ, but I knew better than to obstruct the radio net with needless questions. A few prisoners had passed down the track under escort, sturdy men in their early twenties, some dressed in camouflaged jackets and trousers, others in the long German greatcoats so loved by cartoonists. All wore the cowed and apprehensive air common to the newly-captured.

Then Dutch civilians started to appear. First came an elderly doctor with three female companions who offered to help with the wounded. I directed them towards the dressing station, where they would be welcome. Then a respectable-looking elderly man with a little girl started calmly to roll and stack parachutes, a treasure in nylon and cotton. I felt that I should do something to stop the old gentleman so obviously diverting valuable Government stores towards the Dutch black market, but decided that such officiousness would only be a waste of time. If the man was sent packing, he or others would be back as soon as we had left.

More and more Dutch were arriving, some of them on foot, but most of them riding bicycles. They looked prosperous and well-dressed, probably owners of the comfortable suburban houses nearby. Many were sporting an orange favour – a tie, an armband, or a ribbon – happy in the certainty that the Army of Liberation had arrived, the Boche were beaten and for them the war was over. Everyone seemed to speak fluent English and all wanted to practice it on real Englishmen. A young man on a bicycle, Sten gun slung on his back and sporting a brassard embroidered with the word ORANJE, stopped to chat for a moment before riding away on some unexplained mission. It was the first we had seen of the Resistance. It must have been difficult for them to organize and train in such a thickly populated countryside.

An elderly couple offered us their bicycles, and I accepted the gifts gratefully, at the same time wondering if I should not impound a few more. Useful as the machines would be, it seemed harsh to deprive these pleasant people of their sole means of transport. Then a smooth young man button-holed me with a long tale of Boche brutality; they had requisitioned his motor-car.

Even after four years of German occupation, they seemed to be very innocent. What trouble they would all be in if the battle went the wrong way.

The torpid afternoon dragged by. Slit trenches were dug, but only half-heartedly, because the men knew that orders to move must come at any moment. I could not understand the delay. We ought to have been moving towards Arnhem long ago. What had gone wrong? Yesterday the 1st Para Brigade were to capture the pontoon and the road bridges across the Rhine. Across the latter ran the single main road which linked the city with 2nd Army, sixty miles or so to the south at the start of the battle, and astride this road the Americans were spreading a broad carpet of airborne troops, their 82nd Division securing the bridges over the Waal at Nijmegen and the Maas at Grave; further south still the 101st Division was to seize control of a thirty-mile stretch of road. Up this highway 2nd Army should now be sweeping, their orders being to reach Arnhem tomorrow morning, forty-eight hours after the first airborne landings. By now the glider-borne infantry of the Airlanding Brigade, which had been holding the landing and dropping zones for today's lift, would be marching towards the west of Arnhem to take their place in the left sector of the bridgehead to be formed around the city. Our own Brigade had orders to move in on the right to the Airlanding Brigade to defend the high ground to the north of the city. Tomorrow, the Polish Para Brigade, which had been placed under command of our Division for the battle, would drop on the flat land to the south of the Arnhem bridges and then march north to complete the bridgehead arc.

It was a wide bridgehead, and the Battalion had been given the task of defending a two-mile stretch of it, lying astride the most likely line of approach of a German counter-attack against Arnhem. This was a lot for such lightly armed troops; a frontage of about a thousand yards was all a battalion could be expected to hold against a strong and determined attack. But we would not have to cope alone for very long. By tomorrow evening the 2nd Army should have reached us! After the way the Allies had dashed across France from the Normandy bridgehead, it was unlikely that they would be held up now. In any case the intelligence people at Division had been confident that the Boche had only a few units of third-line troops stationed around Arnhem. Confused and shattered as the enemy were after being chased across Europe, any counter-attack which they might

33

attempt could hardly amount to much. Except, of course, that they would have tanks, and tanks would be difficult to stop in the open parkland north of the city! This was one of the major dangers facing us airborne troops. Our only weapons against armour were the twenty-four guns of the Anti-Tank Regiment, backed up by the short-ranged Piat projectors and anti-tank grenades carried by the parachute and airlanding battalions. To use the latter, one needed to get very close indeed to the tanks, a far from easy problem in the open country in which they would be fighting.

The sight of Captain Jimmy Gray, the Battalion Signal Officer, aroused me from my daydream. A compact, tough little New Zealander, incorrigibly scruffy, Gray had been holidaying in England at the outbreak of war, and had enlisted in a county regiment rather than make the long journey back home to join his own army. After a year with the 8th Army as an NCO, he had been commissioned, and a little later he had joined the Battalion while it was training in Egypt. It had surprised everyone that the Colonel should pick such an untidy individual for his own staff, but the Colonel could choose men. Lucid and quick-thinking, Jimmy's tidy mind belied his appearance.

Jimmy never wasted words. He had come with news. Everything seemed confused, so the Colonel was waiting at his headquarters in case any fresh information arrived. The road bridge in Arnhem had, it seemed, been captured, but was being held only with difficulty. There was very heavy fighting in the western suburbs of Arnhem, where some units of the 1st Brigade were still trying to get through to the bridge. The General, who had disappeared into the town to see for himself what was happening, was missing, possibly killed. One of our own three battalions was already on the move into Arnhem with orders to make for the bridge, while the rest of the Brigade would start in thirty minutes time, at 1700 hours. Casualties in the Battalion had not been light. Two officers and a hundred men had failed to arrive, among them the plane-load which we had seen shot down. Another load had probably been dropped in the wrong place. Ian Hampshire was one of the missing officers; rumour had it that he was dead. The other was the Intelligence Officer, whose job Jimmy Gray had now combined with his own. Jimmy could not explain the reason for the delay. No one seemed to know. Possibly it was confusion caused by the General's absence.

Gray saluted and was away astride his toy motor-cycle, bouncing down the track towards 'B' Company.

When I turned, it was to find the members of my 'O' Group crouched expectantly just beyond the radio. Gray's arrival had alerted them to the fact that something was happening, and they had collected automatically, not waiting to be told to do so. On the right was Robert Watson. Next to him were the three subalterns: Douglas Thompson, Ian Hampshire's close companion, also fresh from school, juvenile in manner but cool in an emergency; fat Leslie Doyle, another founder member of the Battalion, experienced and popular, but lacking that bite needed for promotion; and the much older Luke Tyler, my own contemporary, a sergeant of the Metropolitan Police, a married man with three young children. To the right of the four officers were CSM Huggins and CQMS Bower, both able regular soldiers. It was a sound team.

Private Harrison had already left with orders for the three platoon sergeants to get ready to move. It took me no more than five minutes to repeat what Jimmy had told me, explaining to them that we would move as had already been planned in England, the leading company of the Battalion, with Leslie Doyle's platoon, No. 9, in front, some two hundred yards ahead, followed by company headquarters, then Luke Tyler's 8 Platoon, then Douglas Thompson's 7 Platoon at the back.

As I had expected, the company was ready to move by the time the orders had been given out. Two minutes were all that was needed for the men to slide their entrenching tools into place, pick up their weapons and sort themselves out. No one had removed his equipment. It was a lesson which the Colonel had drummed into us. No man must ever remove his equipment when the enemy were anywhere near, no matter whether he was digging, sleeping or defecating. Whatever time it might be, day or night, a soldier had only to reach for his weapon to be ready to fight or to march. Just once each day, one man in three at a time was allowed to strip so that he could wash and shave. And shave they must.

The last man of 9 Platoon was disappearing round the corner of the sandy track which ran parallel with the railway line to Arnhem when I noticed the Colonel standing on the right next to the shell of a still-smoking glider which partly blocked the Battalion's path. Gray was by the Colonel's side, and behind them crouched a knot of radio operators and orderlies. It was the same as ever. The Colonel's eyes were still, but he never missed anything: the unfastened pouch from which a grenade or Bren magazine could slip; the slack chin-strap which would fail to hold a running man's steel helmet in place. Quietly the Colonel would indicate the error to whichever passing officer or NCO was responsible for the man. Nothing was ever ignored. Safely out of range, the offender would mumble about the nit-picking old bastard, but the abuse was usually perfunctory and good-natured. All of them knew his ways, and by now they had learned that his fads mattered.

36

CHAPTER TWO

ANXIETY

THREE hours had passed and we had covered only six miles. Everything took so long; there was so much delay. First there had been the long wait on the dropping zone, now this slow and irksome march. Already it was dark; the luminous dial of my watch showed nearly half-past eight.

Although we were moving along our planned route, our rôle in the battle had been changed. Instead of making for the high ground north of Arnhem, the whole of the Brigade was now marching for the bridge to relieve the struggling remnants of the 1st Brigade which had been fighting alone there for more than twenty-four hours.

One thing was certain. Parachute infantry were not the fast-moving, hard-hitting troops depicted by the daily press. With no more transport in a battalion than four lightly armoured carriers and some half-dozen jeeps, nearly everything needed in battle either had to be carried on the backs of the soldiers or dragged behind them. There were no trucks just behind the forward companies loaded with spare ammunition; instead, extra bandoliers were slung around necks and light anti-tank mines swung from waist belts. Success came with surprise in this sort of fighting; the enemy must be caught unaware and crushed before they could recover. Inevitably we would run short of ammunition if the Boche were allowed the chance of standing and fighting. This weary trudge towards the bridge in Arnhem along the endless track was a crazy way to use airborne troops. Surprise had been lost long ago. Before the operation started I had doubted the wisdom of dropping so far from the bridges. Now it was clear that it had been a mistake.

Some men carried as much as a hundred pounds on their backs. The most heavily burdened were the 3-inch mortar and heavy machine-gun crews, dragging behind them through the loose sand trolleys laden with their weapons, belts of ammunition and mortar bombs, each weighing ten pounds. And these men of the Support Company were chosen for their size and strength.

Most of the men in the Battalion were in their middle and late twenties. Few were youngsters, and all were hard and fit. In the past we had marched fifty miles in the day over tropical hills, so this evening's work was, by comparison, no more than a gentle stroll. Although they were thirsty, they were used to far worse than this. The water discipline was strict: men drank only when they were given leave to do so, and bottles were never emptied unless water was available to refill them. No one yet seemed to be hungry. We each carried a couple of twenty-four hour ration packs, but I had forced myself to munch an oatmeal bar before leaving the DZ. These bars, which could be eaten cold or crumbled into a tasty and sustaining porridge, were quite the best thing in the packs. Loose in my pocket was a bar of plain chocolate and a few boiled sweets, but these were to be avoided on the march because their sweetness aggravated one's thirst. I had plenty of pipe tobacco and cigarettes also. Was this unexpected weariness psychological? Had the unexpected calmness of the evening, following on the strain and excitements of the day, given us too much time to dwell on bodily discomforts?

For the battle seemed to have rolled away somewhere. As the sun slipped down through the woods behind us, the sounds of firing to the north and east had finally faded. Our boots made no noise in the sand of the track, and no one spoke without cause. The only sounds were the metallic clink of weapon striking bayonet or entrenching tool, the crackle of the radios, or the jargon of figures and words mouthed into the radio sets as officers and signallers tried to keep in contact with one another. Otherwise the night was quiet.

Just before dark, the Battalion halted for a ten minute rest. It was the last chance of a smoke before the next morning and, after clearing the dust from their throats with a short pull at their water-bottles, few men were to be seen without a cigarette between their lips. Non-smokers were rare. On either side of the track, sentries lay alert behind their Bren guns, aching for their turn for a smoke.

The countryside had been monotonous. Even if it had been attractive, it would have been difficult to have enjoyed it. A view was now an analytical problem, not something in which to find pleasure. Ditches were for protection, lanes for movement and hills for observation; hedges and ditches had been placed for human beings, either oneself or the enemy, to hide behind. A landscape was something to be enjoyed in easier times.

This part of Holland had nothing in common with the rest of that flat land. Instead of the rich, level polderland, criss-crossed by dyke or canal, alive with people and their houses, we had been walking through country which was more like the heathlands of Surrey. To the right, we could see little; for most of the time the tall embankment of the Utrecht/Arnhem railway hid everything from view. To the left, there were woods, mostly beech, interspersed with conifers, and divided into geometrical parcels by the rides

39

which intersected them every hundred yards or so. Every so often the trees gave way to open reaches of heathland, similar to the one on which we had landed. Buildings were few, the odd forestry worker's house tucked into the corner of a wood, or a holiday villa in a tidy garden protected by a high wire-mesh fence. The land was not flat, but undulated in green and purple waves which ran up to level ridges from which artillery observers could range their guns. It would be difficult country in which to mount an attack without a lot of fire support.

As the men lay on their backs drawing the last mouthfuls of smoke, down a side track towards us came a small empty farm-cart, drawn by an elderly grey horse and led by an equally elderly Dutch farmer. He was a cheerful little man, exhilarated rather than alarmed by the warlike happenings into which he had stumbled.

Here was the chance to relieve the men of part of their load. In a moment the cart and its driver had been commandeered, and Huggins had passed the word to the platoon sergeants quickly to collect the small packs and dump them on the cart. The Colour-Sergeant was put in charge with orders to keep his eye on the owner and to follow close behind the rear platoon. If we were to clash with the enemy tonight, our burdens would be so much the less. There was nothing in the packs needed for the actual business of fighting, only the impedimenta of living – the rations, mess tins, cardigans, spare socks, and similar odds and ends. The old man showed no concern at the hijacking. Perhaps he was glad to be doing something to help rid his village of the Boche; but, as he spoke no English, there was no way of knowing. Anyway, he showed no signs of worrying.

The Colonel, who had walked up the track to join us as soon as we halted, had been watching the incident with an expressionless face. Perhaps he approved, perhaps he did

40

not, but it was not in his nature to offer advice unless he was asked for it. He left his company commanders alone to get on with the job without interference, provided he trusted them.

A solitary red-bereted officer now appeared, walking down the track from the direction of Arnhem. He was a KOSB captain, belonging to the Airlanding Brigade, and he was on his way to his own Brigade Headquarters on some unexplained mission. Although his news was far from explicit, on one point he was definite: the Germans were holding a defensive position in strength just outside Arnhem astride the Battalion's line of advance towards the bridge. He was able to confirm that the 1st Parachute Brigade was still holding out at the bridge where the casualties had been heavy on both sides, the Germans having already lost 2,000 men, although it was not clear who had counted them.

Leaving the Colonel standing by the side of the track, waiting for his headquarters to overtake him, I walked up to find Doyle and give him the captain's news. He was chatting to Private Jones, the platoon orderly, an artful old soldier, but a likeable man upon whom one could depend in a tight corner.

Doyle was not at all his ebullient self. The task of 9 Platoon was simple. He and his men had to walk straight down the track until they ran into the Boche position. Their first warning of the enemy's presence would be the rifle and machine-gun fire tearing into them. Still less were the two scouts to be envied who would be moving out in front of the rest of the platoon. It was almost inevitable that the first German rounds would hit one or both of them, unless the Germans were cunning enough to let them pass so as to kill more of the men behind. But, without armour in front to draw the enemy fire and pin-point their positions, there was no other way to advance. I had chosen Doyle to lead the advance because I was certain that I could rely on him. This was the penalty for being good at one's job.

When 9 Platoon started forward again, the men were that more tense and alert, now that they knew of the trouble ahead, but they walked more freely, their shoulders relieved of the constricting weight of their packs. They would soon start to slow down, particularly when it got dark, and reluctant though I was to do so, I urged Leslie to get a move on, even though to move quickly was to risk more casualties. Speed was vital if we were to reach the bridge before it was too late.

The last vestiges of daylight had now faded into a black, moonless night. Clouds hid the stars, and anyone leaving a lighted house would have seen only a black curtain in front of him. As it was, our eyes were accustomed to the dark, and could pick out moving figures about twenty feet or so ahead.

As the men of 9 Platoon probed cautiously forward, the rest of the column followed in a series of jerks as the more quickly moving companies and platoons behind overtook those in front; then they had to stop to allow those in front to get ahead again. It was a messy way of moving, tiring too.

It was some fifteen minutes since I had last consulted my watch. For the fifth time company headquarters had overtaken the last man of 9 Platoon, and now I had been standing on the crest of this ridge for at least three minutes, waiting for Doyle's men to get ahead once more. Again I tried to contact him on my walkie-talkie. These were new toys, issued only recently for communication between company commanders and their platoons, or within the mortar and machine-gun platoons. During the day they seemed to work well over short distances, but more often than not they were useless at night. This was one of those nights.

The expected happened. The calm of the night collapsed in an explosion of light and noise. From a wide arc in front of 9 Platoon, streams of white, red and yellow tracer bullets converged on the stretch of track where the men must have flung themselves to the ground. Verey lights and parachute flares, larger and brighter than anything carried by us, swung down towards the earth, lighting the dark countryside to the shade of a grey November morning. A house burst into flames on the other side of the railway. It was too sudden for an accident; the conflagration must have been planned. Anything which moved was now visible. Over all was the noise: the din of shells and mortars, bursting both behind and ahead, merging with the harsh roar of the enemy Spandau light machine-guns and the more sustained drumming of the heavier weapons. Now I could hear another sound. It was the slow rat-a-tat-tat of 9 Platoon's Bren guns and the crack of British rifles replying to the German fire.

This must be the Boche position about which the KOSB captain had warned us. I checked the map, shielding the torch with my body. Yes! It was the Dreijensche Weg, the north–south side road linking the two main highways into Arnhem. It was certainly strongly held; there were a lot of enemy in front of us. The Germans had men everywhere. Not only could they challenge our hold on the Arnhem bridge, but they were also able to oppose the landing of our second lift that afternoon and yet still find men to hold the approaches into the city. I began to doubt the accuracy of the British intelligence estimates of the German strength around Arnhem.

My walkie-talkie was still silent. Somehow I must get forward to 9 Platoon to find out what was happening. I rose to my feet, flinching at the ribbons of tracer which were floating towards the crest of the ridge where I was standing, but dropped again when I saw a single crouched figure

43

running up the track towards me. Then I recognized the broad bulk of Bartholomew, Leslie Doyle's platoon sergeant. This was quick. Leslie had wasted no time in sending back news.

Only a little out of breath, Sergeant Bartholomew sank down by my side and began to speak, his voice as calm and sensible as usual. His leading section had come under fire at a range of only some twenty or thirty yards. It appeared that the Germans had allowed the two scouts to pass unmolested, but everyone else in the front section had been killed. There were several other casualties in the platoon as well, including Mr. Doyle, who had been hit badly in the thigh and was only semi-conscious. The survivors were pinned to the ground by fire which was coming from either side of the track.

This was all wrong. With his platoon commander hit, Sergeant Bartholomew's place was with the platoon. There were plenty of other people to carry messages. Not only that, but Bartholomew could hardly have had time to verify the disastrous information about the leading section. It was far from likely that every man in it had been killed.

So Bartholomew's nerve had broken at the first test. Perhaps the responsibility had been too much for him; whatever it was, he was certainly scared, despite his success in concealing the fact. The sergeant had run away, leaving the platoon to its own devices.

I was flabbergasted. Of all the NCOs, I had judged this cool, reserved man to be the most dependable. A hard taskmaster, too ruthless to be popular, Sergeant Bartholomew had been an effective foil to the easy-going and friendly Doyle, and the two men had formed a fine team. It was incredible that this should have happened.

In the light of a flare, I studied the sergeant's face. There was nothing to be seen. Bartholomew returned my gaze with steady eyes. There could be no point in my further destroying the man's self-respect; it was possible that he might recover after this first shock, his pride taking charge to control his fear.

So my rebuke was restrained, no more than a comment that Bartholomew should have sent Private Jones back with the news and not come himself. Then I stood up once again, told Robert, who had appeared by my side, to take charge, and started down the track towards the forward platoon, motioning Bartholomew to accompany me. There was no need to say anything to Harrison, who automatically rose to his feet, his Sten cradled in his elbow, ready to shoot.

There was a lull now. From time to time one of 9 Platoon's Brens replied to a burst of Spandau fire. There seemed to be three separate guns; if this were so, Bartholomew had certainly exaggerated the number of casualties to the leading section.

From the crest of the ridge, the path ran straight, flanked on the right by the deep railway cutting. At the bottom of the slope the trees ended, thrusting us out into the open into the full glare of the still burning house. Ahead and to the left, the fields rose again towards more trees. We were in the bottom of an open bowl, and I felt very naked. From the flashes of the Brens, the survivors of 9 Platoon were no more than fifty to seventy-five yards away. There was no cover at all. It was odd that the Boche had not yet spotted us. The urge to run the last few yards was overwhelming, but a sharp movement of that sort would certainly attract the enemy's attention.

A burst of Spandau hit the track just behind us, some of the bullets flying high to ricochet off the trees. Instinctively the three of us flung ourselves to the ground as a further gun started to fire straight down the track towards us. The bullets seemed to all but graze my helmet. At last the Boche had spotted our movement; those guns were aiming at us. As we rolled in the dust off the track towards the shelter of a slight bank on the left, it struck me that Sergeant Bartholomew was lucky to have survived his journey back; to have remained with the platoon would really have been safer.

Parachute flares now further lit the bowl, as the firing rose again to the pitch of fifteen minutes earlier. Mortars joined in. A bomb burst some twenty feet behind, showering us with earth and stones as the metal screamed overhead. The amount of ammunition being used by the Boche was astonishing, but luckily much of the firing was very high. They were wasting ammunition, possibly because they were ill-trained or perhaps because they were jumpy. Or both!

There was little chance of reaching 9 Platoon without being hit. In any case, I was in the wrong place here, pinned down like this in the open. I should be with the rest of the company, trying to find a way round this pocket of enemy, although I doubted whether we would be able to make much more progress over strange country in the dark. So long as their ammunition held out, 9 Platoon could hold their own down here and should distract the Boche's attention from the rest of the company.

Telling the other two to follow me, I started to squirm back up the track on my belly, keeping well into the bank on the right. The Boche no longer seemed to be shooting directly at us, but stray bullets still whipped the dust from the surface of the path no more than a couple of yards away. For the first fifty yards or so the going was slow until we were able to stand once again in the shelter of the wood. Bullets were continuing to strike the track, however, and it was a relief to top the crest of the ridge and be welcomed by a waiting and anxious Robert.

When I turned to speak to Bartholomew there was no sign of him. I had last seen him when we had risen to our feet in the wood and had assumed that he was still behind. Surely he could not have been hit without either myself or Harrison noticing? It was with the greatest reluctance that I had to tell Harrison to retrace his footsteps and see if there was any sign of what had happened.

For the moment I had no more time to spare for Sergeant Bartholomew. A few yards away Watson had the 'O' Group ready, waiting for my instructions. It took only a few moments to explain what had happened. Then I ordered Luke Tyler to probe with his 8 Platoon around to the left, but to do no more than try to locate the enemy flank. If the Boche retired, or if none were found, Luke could move up as far as the Dreijensche Weg, but I made it clear to him that under no circumstances was he to try to attack the enemy. If the Boche units were of the low grade type which we had been led to expect, it was always possible that they might take to their heels when they saw Luke coming.

Harrison was back. He had seen nothing of the missing Bartholomew. The sergeant had just vanished. Nothing more was said, but it was plain from Harrison's silence that he had formed his own conclusions.

It took five minutes for Tyler to explain his orders to his three section commanders, who in their turn muttered a few terse words of instruction to their men before they all disappeared down the track into the darkness. Again all was quiet. The flames of the burning house had died away, and the night was dark and silent. Was it possible that the Boche had gone? It was unlikely, but I willed it to be so for the sake of 8 Platoon creeping up that hillside.

After allowing 8 Platoon ten minutes to get clear of the track, I led the rest of the company the same way, back down to the corner of the wood. From there 7 Platoon, now the reserve, was well placed for use in any direction. Also, it was a better place from which to control the battle, although

47

without radio in strange country in the dark any form of control was minimal.

All was still silent. Now was the chance to discover what had happened to 9 Platoon in front, but just as I was telling Watson to work forward to see what he could find, a challenge rang out from the direction of the forward section of 7 Platoon, the voice far too loud. The accent of the reply was familiar, the broad Devon tones of Sergeant Nesbitt, one of Leslie's section commanders, whom a moment later I could just see in the darkness.

Nesbitt had decided that it was time to leave, and had used the lull to bring back the survivors of the platoon. Two men were dead, while nothing was known of the fate of the two scouts. With Nesbitt were five wounded men, two of whom, including his officer, were being carried. Leslie, in shocking pain from a shattered thigh, which morphia had done little to help, had fainted after a few yards and was still unconscious.

A third of the platoon were casualties. It was bad, but not quite as bad as pictured by Bartholomew. I could not blame Nesbitt for withdrawing without permission. Short of ammunition, with their officer wounded and the platoon sergeant unaccountably missing, the men had heard nothing of the troops behind them for the past hour, and had concluded that the Battalion must have pulled back. Nesbitt had seen a lot of war, as his DCM, won in Crete, testified. He understood its muddle; he knew it was rare for a battle to go as planned. His responsibility was to his men, to rescue them from what seemed to be a mess. This he had done, and his judgement had been correct. They were in no place to be caught at daylight, overlooked on a forward slope and encumbered with wounded men.

As Sergeant Nesbitt ended his story, there was an explosion of noise from the north. Again the country shimmered in the light of floating flares. 8 Platoon had also hit the enemy position. Up the hill, the slow chatter of Sten guns was superimposed upon the now familiar din of the Spandaus, tearing the night air like so many pneumatic drills. It was clear that Tyler would make no better progress on the left than Doyle had done down the track.

The light of a flare showed Huggins leading the Colonel towards me from the direction of the railway. It was odd that the CO had not appeared earlier. For the past hour, ever since we had first been fired upon, Robert, as company second-in-command, had been passing a steady stream of information back over the radio. It was unlike the Colonel not to have come to see for himself what was happening.

For all that, I was glad to have been left alone. The muddle would not have pleased the Colonel, although I was at a loss to see how it could have been avoided. It had not been at all a tidy fight; in fact it was still a ghastly mess.

The Colonel answered my unspoken enquiry. The Battalion was out of touch with Brigade; not only had contact been lost on the radio, but an officer who had been sent in a jeep to try to find the headquarters had as yet failed to do so. It was a relief that the Colonel's views coincided with my own. To try to push forward in the dark through strange country against this tough opposition would only lead, first to chaos, and then to disaster. We were, therefore, to halt for the rest of the night and start forward again in the morning when we could see where we were going. The Colonel told me to gather my platoons together and then withdraw them through the covering position which 'B' Company had now occupied along the crest of the ridge where we had halted.

I had worked the problem out in my mind before the Colonel finished speaking. The first task was to contact Luke, away up the hill on the left. Except for the odd single shot or a worried burst of automatic fire, the shooting on that flank had now died away. As I had hoped, Luke was not indulging in unnecessary heroics. We now knew that the northern flank of the Boche position was as strongly held as the centre, astride the track, and I only trusted that 8 Platoon had not lost any men in so obtaining confirmation of the KOSB captain's story.

As the Colonel finished, Private Gregory, who was now acting as Tyler's runner, appeared out of the darkness. The Yorkshireman's message confirmed my reading of the battle. As they emerged from the wood, Luke's men had been fired upon from strongly held enemy positions along the line of the Dreijensche Weg. Two men had been wounded, neither of them seriously, and Luke had then pulled his platoon back into the shelter of the trees. There he was waiting for further orders. Gregory's tale was succinct but complete; he was a well-chosen messenger.

Glancing over my shoulder, I was glad to see that Robert, anticipating the change of plan, had once again gathered the members of the 'O' Group together to receive their orders. A couple of minutes were all I needed to tell the officers and NCOs what to do. Robert, with three senior NCOs, was to get back to the night's firm base and reconnoitre fresh positions. Sergeant Nesbitt, now in charge of 9 Platoon, would follow with the wounded as soon as they were ready to move. 7 Platoon would stay where they were to cover Tyler's withdrawal, while CSM Huggins, with Private Gregory to lead him, would go and bring Luke's platoon back.

As the members of the 'O' Group parted on their separate tasks, I remembered that I had noticed the Colonel walking over towards the tree under which Leslie had been laid. There I found him watching Pritchard who was bandaging and splinting Doyle's thigh. Next to him lay a tall young soldier, 9 Platoon's 2-inch mortarman, who had also been wounded in the leg, fully conscious and in no apparent pain. Doyle's eyes were open but glazed with agony, despite the morphia injection. His lips parted in a ghastly parody of his usual cheerful grin when I spoke. Clearly he had lost a lot of blood. Somehow he must be got back without delay to the Field Ambulance where he could receive proper medical care.

Pritchard had with him a single stretcher on which Leslie could be carried, his thigh immobilized in the Thomas splint. The other man would either have to be carried or supported as well as could be managed. I knew that the Colonel was reading my thoughts. It was a long way. If need be, the two men would have to be abandoned to take their chance by the side of the track. It would be wrong to risk losing other men in trying to get them back.

With Douglas' Thompson by my side, I trudged back down the track along which we had advanced four hours earlier. We were the last two men of 'C' Company. Everything behind was now quiet. It had been a bad start. The Company had done nothing except confirm the KOSB officer's report that the Germans were holding the Dreijensche Weg strongly. To accomplish this had cost us Leslie Doyle and the still absent Bartholomew, while two men in Doyle's leading section were dead and the two scouts were missing, probably either killed or made prisoner. Seven other men had been wounded, including another sergeant. This was a total of thirteen casualties, with another nine men lost when we landed. With nothing at all accomplished, over twenty men had already been killed or injured, and now the Battalion was moving in the wrong direction, back the way we had come. Certainly it had been necessary to escape before daybreak from the deadly bowl of ground in which we had been

51

lying, but why did we have to go back so far. A check of my map by the light of a shaded torch confirmed that the Battalion's firm base was to be more than 2,000 yards back from the place where 9 Platoon had been ambushed. It was a very long way.

Somehow the day had finished very badly. Suddenly I was very weary. From the way young Thompson beside me was stumbling over stones and branches, I knew that he was just as tired. Leslie Doyle would be a sad loss. As a founder member of the company, his happy influence had extended far beyond the men of his own platoon. Also he was a friend, and it was a comfort to have one's friends around one. Both the other subalterns were comparative newcomers, while the rather withdrawn Robert Watson had never been close. Always a little too supercilious, he seemed to guard his privacy behind an impenetrable layer of well-mannered charm.

Presumably 9 Platoon were getting Leslie and the young wounded mortarman back all right. We had seen nothing of them, which was reassuring. It would, of course, have been a waste of time to have ordered Sergeant Nesbitt to abandon them. In the dark the order would have somehow been circumvented. It would take a lot to persuade 9 Platoon to desert Leslie Doyle.

As the track led us over the crest and down the reverse slope of the hill, crouched figures could be seen on either side. We were passing through 'B' Company's position. And then I saw David Unwin. Although I could do no more than distinguish the outline of his bulky figure among the gloom of the trees, before anything was said I could somehow sense his relief at seeing me. We had no time to do more than exchange half-a-dozen sentences, but it was a relief to be told that Leslie Doyle and the other wounded men had indeed passed through ahead of us. With luck, they would have now reached the Regimental Aid Post, where the doctor would be organizing their evacuation to the Field Ambulance and the operating table.

I parted from David, not even having had time to enquire why he was up here with the forward rifle companies. Leaving him there in the darkness of the wood, I realized that, good though it was to be fighting in the company of friends, there was a danger of being distracted by concern for their safety. How hard it must be for brothers serving together in the same unit.

Sooner than expected, we reached the battalion base. It had been sited in a rectangular patch of wood, about twenty acres in size, lying just north of the railway. Guides were waiting to lead us to our positions, where the men of 8 and 9 Platoons were already hard at work, scraping slit trenches in the loose soil with their entrenching tools. Douglas Thompson's platoon sergeant had ready details of the section positions which he had planned, and within five minutes 7 Platoon was also busy getting below ground. I noticed that their recent experience of being mortared had speeded their digging, tired though they were.

I thought about food. For the first time I felt a little hungry. Where was that horse and cart with the packs which held our rations? Nobody seemed to have seen it since the Boche first opened fire. Robert Watson had already checked with Battalion Headquarters, but with no success. So the driver had very sensibly slipped away down one of those many side tracks! In order to save the men a little effort, I had been responsible for losing all their food and their warm pullovers. It was likely to be a very expensive error. I should have known better. Cursing myself for my stupidity, I started to walk around the digging men and was relieved to find that no one else seemed to be thinking about food, although there were plenty of joking references to the acceptability of cups of char and cigarettes, luxuries which in any case were unobtainable in the dark. Only Lance-Corporal Williams's satirical turn of mind was able to extract a little amusement from the situation by dwelling on the little Dutch farmer's good fortune at finding himself the owner of an incredible stock of English tinned food, together with a store of warm clothing, razors and shaving soap.

I found a boiled sweet in a corner of a pocket and sucked it, disgusted by the flavour. It was 2.30 am, a horrible hour, especially so if one is tired, cold and hungry. Thank God it would be starting to get light in about a couple of hours! What would happen tomorrow? Something had gone very wrong indeed. By now we should be dug in on the high ground north of Arnhem, waiting for the Germans to counter-attack the bridges; instead, we were sitting here in the woods, only a few miles from where we had dropped, with strong enemy forces between ourselves and the city, where the men of the 1st Brigade must be fighting for their lives. Wherever one turned, there seemed to be German troops, and good ones at that. The men who had stopped us had not behaved like rear-area troops, scraped together to put up some sort of resistance, but had fought with skill and tenacity.

The slit trenches were dug, and everyone, except for the double sentries in each section and the officers and NCOs on duty, was sound asleep, the men humped like dogs, some curled up with a companion for warmth, lying in their full equipment, their weapons tied to their wrists by the slings. I should be asleep too, not sitting and worrying, feeling sorry for myself, but trying to get some rest in preparation for the coming day. Stand-to would be at 0430 hours, half an hour before first light, when everyone would be awake and ready in his slit, weapon poised for a possible dawn attack.

Telling Williams, who was on duty at company headquarters, to see that I was awakened at 4 o'clock, I curled up on the damp ground and forgot everything.

A hand shook my shoulder. It was Harrison. I had been asleep for just an hour, long enough to ensure a foul awakening. My head ached, my thigh muscles seemed to be paralysed from lying on my pistol, my eyes were gummed up and the taste in my mouth could be washed away only by strong tea, and of this there was none. It was still as dark as ever. I needed to stretch myself, and in any case I must check once again that everything was in order. Telling the sergeant-major, who was taking his turn by the radio, that I was going around the position, I motioned Harrison to follow and set off in the direction of 8 Platoon. Soon the exercise cleared my head and the stiffness vanished, but the taste in my mouth remained. Everything was in order. In each of the nine section positions, the sentries were alert, some standing in their trenches, elbows on the parapets, others hidden in the shadows of trees. None were sitting or lying down. It was another of the lessons which the Colonel had drummed into us. Only a sentry on his feet could be sure of staying awake; once an exhausted man lay down, he was more than likely to drop off, whatever the danger and however hard he might fight against sleep.

By the time I had completed the round of the position and returned to headquarters, the company was stirring. The sentries had awakened the officers and NCOs, who in their turn were shaking the men out of their slumber. Some woke easily; others, usually the younger ones, seemed to be drugged, all but incapable of movement, but in four or five minutes the rustle of movement had ceased. Bladders had been emptied and mouthfuls of stale liquid had been sucked from water-bottles. Now each man crouched in his slit-trench, peering into the gloom and praying for the sun to warm his chilled flesh and for the consolation of a cigarette.

Gradually bushes and trees took shape as the darkness thinned. Only the morning song of a few birds and the occasional half-suppressed cough broke the stillness of the wood. Spread across this quiet countryside, in and among the suburban houses, and far away into the city streets ahead, thousands of men, British and German alike, were crouched like me, loathing the morning, alert for any sign of an enemy creeping forward in the half-light of dawn for a surprise attack.

A few feet away at the other end of the trench a radio crackled and Corporal Galbraith acknowledged a brief message. Before he could whisper the details across to me, I knew what the instructions would be. It was a summons to an immediate 'O' Group at Battalion Headquarters. Something was happening at last. As I hoisted myself to my feet, my mind cleared and the discomforts of the night were forgotten.

With the furthest to walk, I was the last to arrive. As Harrison dropped back to join the group of orderlies and runners chatting in the lee of a small bank of earth, I saluted and slipped into my place in the half-circle of officers and NCOs gathered around the Colonel. It was now light. As I exchanged generalities upon the foulness of the early morning with David, who was sitting on my left, my eyes flickered around the circle of familiar faces. In all there were fifteen of us. As well as the other four company commanders, there were the people in charge of the mortar, the machine-gun and the pioneer platoons. The staff of the Battalion included the Second-in-Command, the Adjutant, Captain Jimmy Gray, and the Intelligence Sergeant, who was standing in for his missing officer. Absent also were Paul Lewis, the carrier platoon officer, and Hugh Elkins, the Quartermaster. The Frenchman had disappeared, but Captain John Simmonds, one of the two FOOs, was there by the Colonel's side.

My eyes came to rest upon the square shoulders of the Regimental Sergeant-Major, who was sitting on the left of the circle, and we exchanged smiles. Nearly everyone was still remarkably neat and clean, despite the fighting of the night before and the traces of the raw earth of the slit trenches on their clothes. But the RSM looked as if he had just emerged from his office on to the parade ground. Every article of his equipment was just as it should be: even his boots were clean, and it was obvious that somehow he had managed to find the opportunity to shave the evening before. He was a guardsman from the Colonel's own regiment, one of those quiet, massive men who rarely raise their voices and whose very appearance inspires confidence. Unless he had been a hard disciplinarian, he could not have done the job, but as was the case with good RSMs, the men liked him, bragging to their friends in other battalions about his unremitting omniscience. He was a shrewd, intelligent Londoner, and it was hard to understand why he had not been commissioned. He would have made a good officer, but good officers were not difficult to find. On the other hand RSMs of his calibre were rare indeed. It was fortunate for the Battalion that promotion had not come his way.

It did not take the Colonel long to give us our orders. The Brigade was to renew its efforts to reach the bridge and bring relief to the men still fighting there. To the north our sister battalion would be advancing parallel with us down the axis of the main road running from Amsterdam into Arnhem, while we were to continue along the line of the railway. The advance of the two units was to be carefully co-ordinated step by step, and our own first task was to capture the

57

wooded Koepel ridge, some three thousand yards short of
the bridge and about a thousand yards beyond the Dreijensche Weg, the road along which we had been stopped the
night before. Information had reached the Colonel that the
Germans had followed up the Battalion's withdrawal during
the night and now held the wooded ridge across which we
had retreated.

Again 'C' Company was to lead, with the task of re-
capturing this ridge, marked on the map by a spot-height of
56·5 metres. 'B' Company, together with the MMGs would
provide covering fire for the initial attack, while 'A' Company was to be held ready to pass through and continue the
assault as soon as Point 56·5 had been taken.

CHAPTER THREE

FAILURE

I crouched on the ground in the cover of the few bushes, scanning the objective through my field glasses for the tenth time. To the right was the railway embankment, below it the rough track along which we had first advanced and then retreated the night before. At the foot of the embankment, and scattered among the bushes which covered its flank, were the humped backs and steel helmets of 'B' Company, ready to give us covering fire. Ahead, the open ground climbed for some six hundred yards towards the edge of the wood where the invisible enemy waited, holding the ridge which we had so pointlessly relinquished the night before. To the left of this wood, the solid farm-buildings of Johanna Hoeve loomed up, as lifeless as the wood itself.

Once again I glanced at my watch. The second hand was about to complete its circuit. It was just 0700 hours. Exactly on time, the leading sections, first of 8 Platoon and then 7, rose to their feet and began the long walk up the open slope towards the enemy. As they did so, the early morning quiet was shattered by the 'B' Company Brens and the heavy machine-guns opening fire from the embankment. Up there, at the edge of the wood, I could see leaves fluttering to the ground from branches gashed by the covering fire, and the spurts of dust leaping from the boles of the trees. Still the enemy gave no sign of their presence. Well disciplined troops, they would be holding their fire until we were closer to them.

When the last men of the two leading platoons were about a hundred yards ahead I followed them, with Harrison alongside me. Robert Watson, with the rest of company headquarters, and Sergeant Nesbitt, with 9 Platoon, still waited in the cover of the bushes, ready to give help where it might be needed.

The leading men were now half-way up the slope, evenly spaced across the field in a pattern all but geometrical. I felt very naked indeed. The rate of fire from the supporting weapons quickened, but still the enemy waited.

The scene ahead brought back memories of fanciful training exercises on the plains of Northern India with troops crossing vast expanses of open ground covered by imaginary fire of palpable insufficiency. The ground ahead today was just as open, and the covering fire was just as inadequate. For this type of attack, a regiment of guns would not have been too much. Those few Brens and machine-guns would never keep down the heads of determined troops well dug in. The covering fire was a joke. This slope was a death trap. Within the next couple of minutes all of us could well be dead or wounded. This was the problem which always faced airborne troops fighting without heavy weapons. We were bluffing. We would survive only if the Boche ran away. They had to be more frightened than we were.

Now the leading men were no more than a hundred yards or so from the edge of the wood. I could see Douglas Thompson's elongated figure on the right, well out in front of his men, clearly the officer leading the attack. Poor kid, he would be the first to be hit. They were so close that the covering fire had stopped for fear of hitting them. All was quiet. Thompson broke into a run, waving to his men to do the same. The Boche must be waiting for this moment. Now they would raise their heads to shoot at us with impunity. It was odd that they had not yet opened fire. Then, down the slope towards me filtered a ragged popping noise. But it was not the enemy. 7 Platoon were firing their weapons from the hip as they charged home. So were 8 Platoon. The leading sections plunged into the wood and disappeared. There were no enemy at all there. The information from Brigade must have been wrong. We had attacked and taken an empty position. Never was there such an anti-climax, but never was anti-climax more welcome.

This morning the walkie-talkie sets were working, but as I grabbed the instrument from Harrison to order the rest of the men forward, I saw that it was not necessary: they were already on their way up the hill. Running forward to the edge of the wood, I met Luke who confirmed that there was no sign of the enemy. He had, however, contacted a KOSB officer whose men had been holding a position just north of Johanna Hoeve. In some amazement the Scots had watched what seemed to be a ponderous and unnecessary assault upon what they knew was an empty wood. It was war's usual muddle.

There was no time to waste. Nesbitt had now arrived with 9 Platoon. In a couple of sentences I saw the sergeant on his way through the two forward platoons towards Point 56·5, some four hundred yards further on up the hill through the trees. Then I told Robert Watson to collect 7 Platoon in reserve to cover the track at the point on the top of the ridge. It was the exact spot where I had met David the previous evening. Five minutes later, Nesbitt's voice came over the radio. He had his objective. I could hear Robert in turn passing this news back to Battalion Headquarters, as I was instructing Luke to get 8 Platoon forward to the edge of the wood and consolidate on Nesbitt's right. Now they were all back where they had been seven hours earlier. What a waste of energy and time!

The Colonel must have anticipated Robert's message, because 'B' Company was already streaming up the slope behind us, making for the position where they were to form up to continue the attack across the Dreijensche Weg towards the Lichtenbeek woods beyond. Harry Bates with 'A' Company was now following 'B' Company up the hill, their task to provide covering fire for the next attack. Then would come the final attack on the Koepel ridge.

There was the sound of a jeep on the track behind. A moment later it came into view, followed about fifty yards behind by a second, which I recognized as the Colonel's. On the bonnet of the leading vehicle flew the small blue triangular flag of the Brigadier.

As the small, spare figure stepped out of the first vehicle, I realized that it was the first time I had seen the Brigade Commander since we left England. He was just the same as ever, relaxed and smiling. Battle was nothing new to him; he had been through the worst of the desert war. Muddle in no way disconcerted him, at least not outwardly. He seemed to anticipate it, understanding how judgement and behaviour were impaired by danger. Wherever he went, he inspired confidence with his gentle eyes and friendly manner. For a regular cavalry officer, his background was unusual. He had come to his regiment, not from Sandhurst but from Oxford with a Double First and fluency in half-a-dozen languages. He wore his learning lightly, as he did his decorations. It was rare for soldiers to be aware of officers more senior than the colonels who commanded their battalions, but every man in the Brigade could recognize and name the Brigadier.

The two visitors did not stay long, but their appearance was a tonic for all. It was a reminder that there were able men in charge, even though the battle was developing in rather an odd manner. Also the Brigadier brought the excellent news that Leslie Doyle was alive and receiving proper medical care in the Field Ambulance. Leslie? It was shaming that I had not given him a thought since early that morning. There was no time to dwell on yesterday. 9 Platoon was now in charge of Nesbitt, and it might ever have been so.

After making a rapid check that Douglas Thompson had his sections in sound positions, I left Robert in charge at company headquarters and set off down the side of the railway embankment to visit the two forward platoons. I was pleased by what I found there. The sentries were well placed and the men were digging hard. At every corner cheerful smiles and jocular greetings met me. The cause of the elation was puzzling. Possibly it was the empty success of capturing an unheld position, or it could have been relief at finding themselves still alive after facing the prospect of imminent death half an hour before. The men were, of course, warm again. The morning's exercise had dispelled the grim chill of the previous night, and now the sun was starting to penetrate the light cloud overhead. It was astonishing to find that it was only a quarter past eight. The day had hardly started.

Then, on the left, the clamour of battle once again erupted. 'B' Company's attack was under way. But now the noise was not just the sound of our own covering fire. From time to time the note of the Brens could be picked out, but the main volume of noise came from German weapons. It was the same as the previous night – Spandaus, heavy machine-guns and mortars, the volume even more intense than before, more so than anything we had heard since we landed.

The noise lessened, to swell again a few minutes later. This happened twice. Then there was silence but for the sporadic burst of automatic fire or a spatter of single rifle shots. I could make nothing of the sound except that 'B' Company's attack, unlike our own, had met trouble; there was no indication of success or failure. They were attacking in the cover of the trees, not over the naked ground which we had faced, but the sound of the German fire was terrifying in its intensity.

I was nervous for news, but up here with 9 Platoon I was unlikely to receive any. The walkie-talkies had not worked well since we entered the woods, and in any case the range to company headquarters was too great. Again I was in the wrong place, too far forward, out of touch with my communications.

In less than ten minutes I was back at company headquarters. Robert was on the set, his helmet thrown to one side, his long legs twisted beneath him in the cramped confines of the slit trench. The earphones framed a stubble-covered face, the features strained with the concentration of trying to pick up the half-heard messages passing between the other two rifle companies and battalion headquarters, and at the same time translating the words and figures from code into plain English by means of the green Slidex pad spread open on his lap.

Robert noticed me standing above him and lifted the earphones from his head so that he could answer the unspoken question. The noise swelled once again to a crescendo, but now it sounded rather further away. There was little to learn. Interference on the wireless net was so bad and the distance so great that he had managed to pick up only snatches of information. It seemed that 'B' Company's attack had been stopped, but before Robert could establish this for certain the 'B' Company set had gone off the air. 'A' Company was trying to make progress to the north, around 'B' Company's left flank, and the fire which we could hear must be the German response to this attack. It sounded most unpleasant.

Suddenly my preoccupation with the problems of others ceased. There was a familiar whine overhead, and I found myself propelled into the half-dug trench, all but on top of Galbraith and Robert. The action had been a reflex. I knew that I had made no conscious decision to jump. As I lay there with my second-in-command's entrenching tool carving a ridge into my left buttock, the mortar bomb burst about eight feet to the right. The scream of the shards of jagged metal passing just overhead flailed my ears, as earth and stones spattered down on top of us. The stench of high explosive filled the trench.

My face, I found, was pressed into the coarse material of Corporal Galbraith's battledress trousers. Gingerly raising my head, I peered over the low parapet. At the foot of a tree, some fifteen yards away, lay a motionless heap, a green and khaki bundle which did not stir. Jumping out of the trench, I ran across and turned the limp body over. The head fell back to show the open, staring eyes of Sergeant Hawkes, one of the 7 Platoon section commanders, a bright young NCO, only just promoted, who had been with the Battalion since the day it was raised. He was another old friend. At first I could see no sign of any injury, but then I noticed the small hole in the back of Hawkes' helmet and the thin stream of blood streaking the back of his neck.

Again there was the whine, but this time it was more than the one bomb. As I dived towards CSM Huggins' trench, which was closer than the one I had just left, I was conscious that I was now in control of my own momentum. The first shock must be over.

Lying by Huggins' side, I seemed to count seven explosions, all just a little further away than the first, but still close enough to smell the hot gases. There was a short pause, and then, as if it were an afterthought, an eighth bomb struck the branches of the tree just above us, directing its hot metal splinters down into the trenches below. A half-strangled cry of distress brought my head up, just in time to see Corporal Pritchard clamber out of his slit and race across towards the cry, his haversack of medical supplies, marked with its red cross, dangling from his hand

The pause lasted no more than half a minute. Again the whine; again I ducked. Was this the covering fire for a counter-attack, or were the Boche merely harassing us spitefully? But when I raised my head from Huggins' boots to look around, it was a relief to see one of the 7 Platoon Bren gunners, his helmet and eyes just above the level of the parapet, gazing down the track towards his front. So the sentries were still doing their job; the fire was not forcing down their heads. If this was the covering fire for an attack, we would not be caught unawares.

The mortar fire was shifting, falling further forward towards the trees where the other two platoons were lying. Away to the north, the noise of battle from the other side of the Battalion area continued undiminished, but now there was a fresh sound, overlaying the persistent rumble of guns and mortars. Out in front, ahead of 8 Platoon, the throb of powerful engines, racing at times, warned of a fresh threat – it was some type of armoured vehicle, an SP gun or a tank.

The lull provided the chance to finish the digging. I shouted an order, and within the minute all of them, except for the sentries, were out of their holes, their entrenching tools shifting the soft earth with the speed of a squad of Geordie miners. Harrison and I had been away visiting the forward platoons when the digging started, so we had no hole of our own, but now the two of us began to put this right, working even faster than the men around us to carve our niche in the ground.

66

Those who had dug deep enough were roofing their trenches to provide some protection against the tree-bursts. Small branches covered with about a foot of earth served well, but by the side of the track one of the 7 Platoon sections had found a dump of cut poles, a rather more satisfactory building material. There was no longer any need to persuade the men to dig faster; the lesson had really been driven home. They had learned that anyone lying in a slit-trench had little to fear from mortar bombs, other than a direct hit, and the odds against that were long. The danger came from the plunging metal of the bombs bursting in the tree tops. In the recent bombardment only two men had been hit: Sergeant Hawkes killed in the open, away from his trench, and the second man, hit by a tree-burst, who had suffered only a painful wound in the backside.

We had been digging for no more than a few minutes when the sound of firing to the north slackened. But the noise from the vehicles in front had increased. The thud of guns only a few hundred yards away was punctuated by the hammering of Brens. Both forward platoons were in action, and I had placed company headquarters too far back to be able to see what was happening. The walkie-talkies were silent. Also, I was worried about the siting of the platoons, some three hundred yards apart, each isolated in its own corner of the woods and unable to support the others against a determined attack. It was too late to move anyone at this juncture, just when the battle seemed to be hotting up, but I had to know what was happening. It would be wrong to visit the forward platoons myself at this juncture when fresh orders might at any moment be passed over the radio. Robert would have to go.

No sooner had his long legs disappeared around the corner of the track towards 8 Platoon, his diminutive runner,

Private Robertson, following, than a burly figure approaching from the direction of the other forward platoon caught my eye. It was Sergeant Prior, one of Nesbitt's section commanders, a rather sulky man, able and well-educated, but with a grudge against authority. In his left hand Prior grasped his Sten in a grip so firm that the knuckles showed blue under the sunburn; his right arm, from which the clothing had been cut away at the shoulder, was thrust into the front of his smock, the elbow covered by a blood-stained dressing. His face was white with shock and taut with pain. A morphia injection was doing little to alleviate the agony of an elbow smashed by a bullet.

The news Prior brought was serious. The vehicles which we could hear were Boche armour, driving backwards and forwards along the road and sweeping the front of 9 Platoon's position, secure from retaliation. Other than anti-tank grenades, the only armour-piercing weapons carried by the company were the small Piats, tripod-mounted projectors which threw a hollow-charged bomb some hundred feet, far too short a distance to hit the armoured vehicles which were shooting at us from a range of several hundred yards. So far the armour had claimed only Prior, but Sergeant Avondale had been killed by a mortar fragment as he dashed across between a couple of trees to put some question to Nesbitt.

I really did dislike Prior. In pain though the man was, he still managed to introduce a nuance into his voice suggesting that his wound and Avondale's death were somehow the result of their company commander's mishandling of the situation. I was ashamed that I could feel no sympathy at all for him. Hard though I had tried, I had never been able to discover the reason for this animosity. It was a relief to see the man's back disappearing down the track in the direction of the Field Ambulance.

But this inexorable loss of skilled leaders was serious. In our parachute battalions, unlike the usual infantry units, section leaders ranked as sergeants, not corporals. 9 Platoon had now lost not only its officer, but three of its four sergeants as well. Hawkes was dead, and one of 7 Platoon's section commanders had failed to appear at the RV after the drop. Already nearly half the sergeants had become casualties.

Still there was no news from battalion headquarters. Rigid in his trench, his features strained into a mask of concentration, Corporal Galbraith was trying to catch the ever fainter sounds which percolated over the air into his headphones, but the batteries which powered the set were all but dead, and the last of the spares had been used. How vital such small things could be! With no radios the further the companies and platoons were spread across the countryside, the more difficult it became to control the battle.

Wireless batteries, food, water and ammunition: the four requisites for survival! The batteries were finished; we could exist for a time without food and water. But ammunition we must have, and this was becoming scarce as well. We must get more soon or we would be finished.

There was no pattern to the enemy fire. Their mortars would search up and down the railway line, before swinging again to the edge of the wood where the two forward platoons lay. Or a fifteen minute silence would be followed by a hail of bombs directed into an area empty of our troops. Then suddenly the bombs would be bursting above and around us once again. In the same way the sound of the armour out in front seemed to drift aimlessly from one flank to another, the long bursts of fire from the machine guns and the Spandaus rasping from side to side. Certainly the Boche were not short of ammunition. For every round which we heard fired by our own rifles and Brens in front, at

69

least twenty seemed to be coming from the other direction.

Robert was away for about forty-five minutes. The news he brought back confirmed Sergeant Prior's report. Avondale was certainly dead, and two more members of 8 Platoon had been wounded by mortar fragments, neither seriously; both men were staying with the platoon for the time being. There was little to be seen in front. The Germans were well concealed; only the occasional flash of one of their weapons provided a target at which to shoot. On the left the thick woods blocked any sight of the savage battle which 'A' and 'B' Companies had been fighting against the enemy holding the line of the Dreijensche Weg. The armoured cars were a nuisance, but a danger only if one had to expose oneself. This, of course, Robert had been forced to do as he moved from section to section along the front, but to provide an account of his personal adventures was beneath his dignity. Robertson, however, was less reticent. Twenty feet away, he could be heard giving his friends a blow-by-blow description of what had clearly been an unpleasantly dangerous tour.

Two things were encouraging. Robert's report had confirmed what I had guessed from the noise of the battle. The men in the two forward platoons were not wasting their precious ammunition. Fire discipline was sound; they were shooting only when they could see something to shoot at. Secondly, the cover which they had built over their slit-trenches was not only protecting them from the mortar bombs bursting in the trees but was giving them confidence. Like myself, most of them had cowered when the first bombs fell among their half-dug trenches. Now men seemed to be taking their time before ducking their heads under cover, as the whistle of yet another batch of falling bombs blasted their eardrums.

After we had put the final touches to our slit-trenches, time was found to scrape a shallow grave for Sergeant

70

Hawkes. It was hard to suppress one's revulsion at touching the body of someone I had known so well, but just as I was steeling myself to do so, Huggins stepped forward, ripped open the dead man's smock and shirt and slipped one of the two identity discs over the blood-stained head. The sergeant major then unbuckled his watch and searched the pockets for anything which might be useful: a morphia syringe and a field-dressing, a bar of chocolate and a couple of Mills grenades, two packets of cigarettes and a box of matches, a couple of maps and a pocket-knife. There was nothing personal except for a grubby envelope containing half-a-dozen faded and dog-eared snapshots of a stout, smiling girl holding a baby. Before buttoning the envelope into his breast pocket, Huggins slipped the identity-disc between the photographs.

I was helping Corporal Pritchard shovel the earth back over Hawkes' body, listening with one ear to Huggins sharing the dead man's ammunition and other possessions among the members of company headquarters, when suddenly I became aware of Jimmy Gray standing beside me, apparently anxious to speak but diffident at interrupting. Telling Pritchard to finish the job, I rose from my knees, glad to be able to put my mind to something else.

When I turned to speak to Gray I was disturbed by what I saw. The dirt of battle had exaggerated his usual scruffiness. His smock and trousers were coated with mud and dust and his right sleeve was stained from top to bottom with blood – not his own, as he explained when he saw my eyes fixed on it. The front of his smock and the battledress jacket underneath had been torn by a large fragment of mortar bomb, which in some miraculous fashion had failed even to scratch him; three inches to one side and it would have severed his head. But it was the eyes above the pallid, unshaven cheeks which were frightening. They were empty of life. When he

71

spoke, the words were as lucid and well-chosen as ever, but the voice lacked expression. The phrases were cold. It was not as if he were describing events which he had himself witnessed, but something unreal, something half-imagined.

'B' Company had attacked at 0800 hours. At the start their advance through the woods had gone like the first attack of the morning, a calm and steady progress against a seemingly non-existent enemy. Then, some hundred yards short of the Dreijensche Weg, a swathe of fire had cut down the men of the two leading platoons. The half-grown trees and the sparse undergrowth had neither hidden them nor shielded them from the interlocking arcs of the enemy weapons which covered every inch of ground. It was just possible that they might have been able to deal with the machine-guns alone, but the armour was too much for them, pumping shells into the men at near point-blank range.

Gray had seen it all happen. The Colonel had tried to stop the attack as soon as the full strength of the enemy position had become clear but by then more than half the men of the two leading platoons had been killed or wounded. Both subalterns were dead; the other officers and the CSM had all been wounded.

The Colonel had then tried to turn the German flank by sending 'A' Company round to the left. But there was no flank. The second attack had been a replica of the first. It too had collapsed, but not before some forty more men were dead or maimed, including two of the four surviving officers. Harry Bates himself had been horribly wounded in the stomach and by now was probably dead. As Gray had pulled him behind some cover, his blood had soaked his sleeve.

This was not the complete story. There was further bad news. Not only had our own attack been shattered, but the other battalion to our north had hit similar enemy positions

72

and was making little progress in its efforts to get into Arnhem along the main road. From somewhere or other the Boche had found enough troops of a quality good enough to smash the Brigade's attempt to reach the city.

Lightly equipped as we were, without armour, guns or aircraft to help us forward, we would never manage to take a position as strong as this one. Surprise was the main supporting weapon of airborne troops, and this had failed us. The Boche had stopped us reaching the bridge.

I listened in silence to Jimmy Gray's measured words, feeling little emotion. He might have been talking about strangers. For a moment I felt sick at the description of Harry's injuries, but otherwise the story of disaster did not seem to touch me. Aware that this should not have been so, I wondered at my state of mind. I knew them all so well, even those who had only recently joined the Battalion. Many were long-standing, close friends. And now they were lying in those woods on the other side of the hill, savagely maimed or dead, and I could stand here listening dispassionately to Jimmy Gray's story. What was wrong? Was it just that, unlike Jimmy, I had not seen it all happen? Or could it be relief that my own company had been spared the worst? Or was my mind so filled with the problems of my own men that I had no capacity to spare for the sufferings of others?

Gray was still talking. At any moment the Germans might counter-attack, and the Colonel was trying to sort out the chaotic aftermath of the morning's fighting, overseeing the digging of trenches and the evacuation of the wounded so as to be ready for the enemy when they came. My own company was to hold on in their present area, while the rest of the Battalion dug in on the other side of the hill 9 Platoon was defending.

The news could hardly have been worse, but at least the

uncertainty had been dispelled. Now that the situation was clear, I could do something about it.

First everyone must learn what had occurred before rumours even more alarming than the truth started to reach them. A quick word with Robert and Douglas, and then I set off in the direction of the two forward platoons, carrying spare radio batteries, a supply of which Gray had brought with him.

The route to 9 Platoon was now quite familiar, but I approached the position with care, wary not only of enemy snipers but also of our own men, possibly trigger-happy, who might react just that bit too quickly to the sight of two figures appearing out of the trees behind them. The men of the rear section did, as it turned out, see Harrison and myself before we spotted them, and the Bren gunner called us softly over. It was a relief to discover how effectively the platoon had managed to roof and camouflage their trenches before the armour pinned them to the ground. In front one could just manage to distinguish Sergeant Nesbitt's trench at the foot of a large tree.

Telling Harrison to stay where he was, with some trepidation I crawled across the thirty yards of open ground towards Nesbitt. Nothing happened until I was just lowering my legs into the trench, squeezing down by the sergeant's side. Then a burst of Spandau cracked past, cutting a shower of twigs and leaves from the branches of the tree overhead. As I ducked inside the trench, I felt it necessary to apologize to Nesbitt and Private Jones, his runner, for attracting enemy fire on to their position.

I started to tell the sergeant the news, but was distracted by a novel sound, one that I had not heard before in Holland. From far away in the distance came the drum of powerful aeroplane engines. Nesbitt was the first to spot the minute shapes, first circling and then diving out of the sun towards

74

us, the noise changing to a shriek as the machines swept down towards the woods. From half a dozen different directions a happy shout of 'Spitfires' rose from the trenches. At last some help had arrived from the outside world. The RAF had arrived to give us close support.

As I gazed up at the dozen Spits screaming down to strafe the Boche positions on the sloping ridge ahead, Nesbitt's voice suddenly roared in my ear, shouting to everyone to get their heads down and hide their faces. As I ducked with the rest, I spotted the black crosses on the wings. The aircraft were not ours, but German Messerschmitts. Our air superiority was so overwhelming that it had never occurred to anyone that the machines might be hostile. They were not diving on to the enemy positions but on to our own. Somehow or other the Boche had scraped a few aircraft together to fling into the battle.

Although I knew that a face, even one as dirty and sunburnt as my own, could be spotted with ease from an aircraft, I could not resist lifting my head for a moment to peer at the machine immediately overhead. My face shielded by the sleeve of my smock, I gazed skywards. The Messerschmitt was so close that I could see the pilot's face. Two rockets detached themselves from its wings and swooped down to explode seconds later in the woods where the survivors of 'A' and 'B' Companies, were settling into their new positions. Aircraft recognition had never been my strong point, but I should have noticed that they were not British planes. Sergeant Nesbitt, who had survived the continuous dive-bombing of the Battle of Crete, must have developed a keener sense of danger.

As I ducked once more, there was another scream of engines behind, followed by the sound of a storm of bullets striking the branches of the trees on either side. Two aircraft which had discharged their rockets were now carrying out

75

a second run, strafing with their machine-guns. As I squeezed even closer to the earth at the bottom of the shallow trench, the reverberations of an explosion some fifty yards away pounded my eardrums. It was another rocket.

Suddenly it ended. There was silence. Silence, for the first time that day. The aircraft had vanished as quickly as they had arrived, and even the troops on the ground had stopped firing. We were still at the bottom of our slit trenches, while the Boche were either sheltering too, or had just stopped firing to watch the show.

Something made me glance at my watch. Long day though it had been, it was still only 11 o'clock. It was hard to believe that we had been in Holland for only twenty-four hours. I stood up, releasing Sergeant Nesbitt, who had been trapped underneath me.

After Nesbitt had checked his three sections, I learned with surprised relief that no one had been hurt. The Germans had used a lot of high explosive in this corner of the wood to no effect at all. It seemed unlikely that we had escaped so easily elsewhere.

The mortars started once again as I set off with Harrison towards 8 Platoon. In a few moments the harsh roar of the battle, swelling in from every direction, once more engulfed us. So long as one was below ground level, the flurries of jagged metal, showering down from the trees or driving horizontally at the parapets of the trenches could be borne. We were accustomed to it now. But out here there was nowhere to hide. We lengthened our step towards the place where we hoped to find 8 Platoon. What quantities of ammunition the enemy were able to squander, and how helpless we were without the means to retaliate. We had yet to hear even our own mortars firing. As only such a minute quantity of ammunition could be dragged along the sandy tracks in the two-wheeled trollies, the Colonel was probably keeping our stocks in hand for the inevitable German counter-attack.

Out here in the open without proper anti-tank protection, how were we to fight off the enemy armour? What had happened? In less than a day we had been beaten on to the defensive. But at least the 1st Brigade was still hanging on at the bridge and tomorrow the 2nd Army should arrive.

At the edge of the wood, just above the point on the track where we had first come under fire last night, I caught sight of Luke Tyler, hunched up behind a tree in animated conversation with Sergeant Weiner, the junior of his section commanders. The subject being discussed was Weiner's Bren-gun position, which was sited to cover the open bowl of ground in front of 9 Platoon on the left. From their gestures, it appeared that Tyler did not approve of the fashion in which the trench had been camouflaged. Weiner was volubly defending his section's work, his swarthy features as alive with the argument as a Petticoat Lane trader extolling the quality of his wares on a summer Sunday morning. Luke's impassive policeman's face gave nothing away. In the end he would have his way, and Weiner would do what he was told after the routine protest. The two men respected one another.

I would have liked to have known Luke better. One of our last-joined reinforcements, he had only been with the Battalion for about three months. Commissioned a short time before, and cautious by nature, he had approached with some care this new world of the Officers' Mess, inhabited by a collection of people most of whom had known one another for several years. As he felt his way along, he had shown that he knew his job, and had gained the confidence of his platoon with reassuring ease. During the past week, when everyone had been busy making ready for the operation, his reserve seemed to be on the point of collapse, but

77

now he appeared to have built his defences once again as if to insist that he should prove himself before asking for acceptance.

In fact 8 Platoon was in sound hands. This the soldiers knew, and I knew it as well. I was wondering how it could be made clear to Luke, without embarrassing both of us, that he had long since earned his place in the company, when the distant sound of aeroplane engines once again obtruded over the noise of the battle. But this time the note was altogether different, the measured solid throb of a fleet of large aircraft flying in formation. Then, to the south of us, across the top of the rail cutting, I saw the familiar shapes of a line of Dakotas, approaching at about 1,000 feet. In a minute the sky was crammed with them.

It was the first supply drop, about which we had been told at the briefings. But the DZ was a couple of miles away, over the other side of the hill, right in the middle of the enemy positions. By now, of course, the Division should have captured the area, but the Boche still held it. News of the progress of the battle could not have reached the RAF, or the pilots would have been diverted to drop their supplies elsewhere. Did this mean that contact had broken down with the rest of the army on the other side of the Rhine?

Already the Dakotas were in trouble. Multiple explosions from the enemy light ack-ack guns hammered from every direction, and the results were visible in the black, circular bursts which seemed to all but fill the gaps between the ranks of aircraft. But not all were missing their targets. One plane exploded in a ball of fire to vanish behind the trees. And then, as the first aircraft passed over our heads, the parachutes started to open, carrying the ammunition and food which we so desperately needed right into the middle of the German positions.

The battle on the ground seemed again to be in suspense.

Even the enemy mortars had stopped shooting. Regardless of the danger, some of 8 Platoon were on their feet, waving their weapons or helmets, or the small yellow squares issued for the purpose, trying to attract the attention of the pilots. Others seemed to be mesmerized by the spectacle – the solid aircraft and the men inside so pointlessly being destroyed. Away on the far side of the bowl, along the edge of the wood, I could see two small German guns pumping their shells into the sky, the minute grey-clad figures busy beside them. A Bren stuttered. Weiner had spotted the gunners as well, but the range seemed to be too great. Still the guns continued to pour out their shells.

Perhaps the crews were so intent on driving forward through the flak to find the DZ and drop their stores that they never saw the waving men. Perhaps they thought that the Germans were trying to mislead them. Whatever it was, the procession thrust steadily on, dropping the supplies away in the distance, well beyond us. The sky was now full of aircraft, some pounding forward in rigid formation, others diving in flames to left or right, or peeling away in distress to try to find a way back to base.

Among the mass, a single Dakota just overhead caught my attention. It had already been hit and flames were creeping down from the starboard engine towards the cockpit. As it lost height, the khaki-clad RASC despatchers were standing at the open doorway, pushing out the panniers of supplies. I could see their faces. The fire was on their side of the plane; the wing was burning before their eyes.

The Dakota was now little more than 300 feet above the ground. If the men at the door jumped now, they might just save themselves. In a second or two more the aircraft would be so low that their parachutes would not have time to open.

This the men must have known, but they went on with their routine drill, pushing out the panniers regardless of what would happen to them. Then the starboard wing crumpled. The flaming plane disappeared beyond the trees, the panniers still falling from the open door.

The sky was empty. The last plane had gone. But we still stood watching the place where the Dakota had vanished, mourning the futility of the self-sacrifice we had just witnessed.

Two hours later the memory of the RAF crew and the RASC despatchers still nagged through my other cares.

The rest of the Battalion had now formed a firm base around the hill, so that it had been posible to pull back 9 Platoon to some fifty yards in front of company headquarters, where the sections had dug fresh positions. The company was now more compact, better able to withstand the coming German attack. But still there was no sign of the enemy making a move. They seemed content to wait and watch. The machine-gun and rifle fire continued, but the mortars were quiet. On the other hand the sound of gunfire from the north-west, from over my left shoulder was disconcerting. Were the Boche all round us now?

Only two more men in the company had been hit since the abortive supply drop, but both of them were sergeants from 8 Platoon, and both had been shot by snipers. One had been wounded only slightly through the shoulder, a simple flesh puncture, but the other had been carried back unconscious with a smashed cheek and eye. This steady drain of leaders was becoming ever more alarming. Well over half the sergeants had now been killed or wounded and the sections were in charge of junior NCOs. Wondering to myself if the Boche could spot the badges of rank sewn on the sleeves of their airborne smocks, I realized that there was little point in wearing the things. Everyone in the company knew everyone else, so the stripes were nothing more than identification aids for the snipers. There was no way of avoiding officers and NCOs attracting attention. With their orderlies, they were always on the move. Where the trouble was, there they had to be, and, by nature of the job, they had to wear other distinguishing marks such as map cases and binoculars slung around their necks. Anything was worth trying to stop the slaughter, so I turned to Huggins and told him to send out an order to the platoons for all officers and NCOs to remove their badges of rank and throw away map cases; maps should then be stuffed into pockets and binoculars pushed inside the necks of smocks.

As I watched Robert slip his captain's stars off his shoulders and tuck them away in a pocket, I knew for certain that my second-in-command disapproved. Officers should show themselves as such!

From the corner of the woods where our headquarters was concealed, there was a clear view of the open ground over which the company had carried out its superfluous attack early that morning, so very long ago. The wide stretch of farmland sloped gently up towards the main Amsterdam road, with the Johanna Hoeve farm buildings just visible through the trees some three hundred yards to the north. Some of the KOSB were still in these buildings, but they were not visible. At some time during the day I should have made contact with the Scots, either visiting them myself or sending Robert, but we had been altogether too busy. This was the very first time we had been able to draw breath. In any case the KOSB officer could well have come down to contact us.

It looked so peaceful. Nothing moved. Even the racket seemed to be subsiding, except away in the north, where the rest of the Scots must be, over in those trees towards the main road. I did not like it.

81

Anyway, for the time being the mortaring had stopped, so it was possible to relax for a few minutes in the shade of a tree just behind my slit trench. I felt in my pocket for a boiled sweet, and could find only the one. The bar of chocolate had gone long ago. Our last proper food had been the sandwiches on the airfield well over twenty-four hours ago, but this was the first time I had really noticed the lack of food. I decided to keep the last sweet for the evening. Filling a pipe instead, it was good to be reminded that my tobacco pouch was full and my cigarette case less than half empty.

The voice of Sergeant-Major Huggins recalled me from my reverie. The Colonel was coming, driving down the track from the direction of 9 Platoon. A warning had arrived over the walkie-talkie at the moment Huggins caught sight of the vehicle, into which were crammed not only the driver and the Colonel, but also Jimmy Gray, a radio operator and three men of the Colonel's bodyguard. There was a slight note of alarm in Huggins' voice, detectable only to someone who knew him very well indeed, as there would have been if the Colonel had walked unannounced into the company billets in England, his eyes alert for offending details. Huggins made a rapid survey of the headquarters' trenches, and a rasping rebuke descended upon the unbuttoned pouches and hanging chin-strap of the luckless Private Jackson, a good soldier, but a sloppy looking man, always untidy. There seemed to be nothing else to criticize.

I walked over to meet the Colonel, taking the pipe from my mouth so that I could salute. The two of us sank down behind a tree; the Colonel was not the man to attract attention to a position by standing about in the open. He had little time to spare. The news he brought was not good. Our other battalion's attack had failed as badly as our own, while behind the Brigade what appeared to be a strong German force was pushing south in the direction of Wolfhezen, a

82

prosperous suburban village just south of the railway embankment and some three thousand yards to our rear. The only crossing point over the railway lay at Wolfhezen, and if the Germans were to seize the place, the Brigade's vehicles would be trapped north of the railway. Because of this the Brigadier was sending the other battalion back to hold it.

The Colonel went further. He thought it more than likely that we in our turn might have to pull back, and with this in mind he was issuing tentative orders for a withdrawal in case we had to move. The details of timings and bounds were complex, as was always the case when carrying out that most difficult operation of war – the perilous manoeuvre of disengaging in daylight from an enemy who can see you and is shooting at you.

The Colonel had wasted no time. Less than ten minutes after arriving, his jeep was disappearing up the track, weapons protruding in every direction like a scene from a comic gangster film. He had told us what to do, found time for a cheerful word with everyone in sight, and had gauged the state the company was in.

Again it was necessary to remind myself of the need to guard against allowing my doubts to percolate to the men. It was clear to me what was happening, but, as I looked around, all that I could hear was a hum of cheerful chatter. Although the Colonel had brought bad news, few seemed to realize how bad it was, and his visit had in some strange way released a flow of fresh confidence among those who had spoken to him.

Again there was that familiar noise above us – the throb of aircraft engines once more. Now the planes were flying rather higher, and each one was towing a glider, as large as the aircraft itself. As before, flak was bursting around the lumbering shapes, but now with less effect. Possibly the range was greater and the planes were flying high enough to

avoid the small-arms fire. On they came. None fell out of
the sky. Then, just overhead, the first of the gliders separated
from its tug, banking steeply as it did so before swooping
like some improbable bird, straight down towards the spot
where we lay.

Only then did I remember that the glider-borne part of
the Polish Parachute Brigade was due to land that afternoon
upon the stretch of open country below us, at the same time
as their parachute battalions were dropped in the polderland
south of the Arnhem bridges, but I half-recollected having
been told that it had all been cancelled because the Boche
still held the dropping zones.

In the distance some figures were moving towards us
across the fields upon which the gliders were about to settle.
A Spandau opened up from the woods, and two dropped.
They must be part of our other battalion, withdrawing
towards Wolfhezen. So the landing zone was already a
battle-field and the wretched Poles were about to land into
the middle of it!

The first of the gliders hit the ground, its massive weight
tearing up chunks of stubble as it skidded to a halt, lurching
on to one wing as it did so. Men jumped out and rushed to
the rear to release the tail unit so that the vehicles inside
could be driven out. Two more gliders were now ploughing
across the ground. Another exploded in the air in a vast ball
of yellow flame just as it was upon the point of touching
down. Mortar bombs were bursting among the men struggling to release their loads, while streams of tracer bisected
the scene into oddly formal patterns. Another glider was on
fire on the ground, as still more swooped in to land, adding
to the chaos. One load at least was clear: a jeep towing a
6-pounder anti-tank gun bounced across the uneven surface
towards Johanna Hoeve. The Poles were now joining in the
battle themselves, some firing towards the Germans, some

84

towards the KOSB and some in the direction of our other battalion. It must be impossible for the Poles to distinguish enemy from friend; they probably thought that they had landed into a circle of Boche units, all intent upon their destruction.

In only a few minutes it was all over. From the wrecked and flaming gliders which now littered the ground, small parties of Poles were making their escape, firing at anything they saw move. Two or three vehicles had been driven away, but otherwise they had failed to drag their jeeps and guns from the gliders. The Polish anti-tank battery no longer existed as a fighting unit. It had landed in the middle of a battle and been destroyed before it could fire a single shot. Waste! It was waste once again! Waste, like the supply drop! Nothing seemed to go right.

A knot of some eight Poles charged towards us, intent on seeking shelter, either in the woods or behind the safety of the railway embankment. Some thirty yards away, one man, slightly ahead of the others, must have noticed our camouflaged steel helmets in the slit trenches ahead and shouted a warning. In a bunch they flung themselves into the undergrowth.

Anticipating what would happen, I yelled to everyone to get their heads down, just as a hail of bullets from the Poles whistled over our heads, a few hitting the trench parapets, but most striking the trees well above our heads as the excited men emptied their weapons in our direction.

So long as we kept our heads down we were safe from the Polish fire, but the worry was that some of them might creep closer and start to fling grenades around. However, in a couple of minutes the firing slackened, and then ceased. Possibly the Poles sensed that something might be wrong when no one retaliated. The comparative silence provided the opportunity to shout a warning across the narrow stretch of ground which separated us. There was no reply and I shouted once again. In faltering English a voice enquired who we were. Firmly, CSM Huggins told them. The Poles seemed to understand. After a few seconds of audible consultation, they rose to their feet and walked across. Now that they were for the moment safe, they found the situation funny, but it was a joke which we failed to share.

Only one of the Poles could make himself understood in English, the man who had replied to my shout, a large and enthusiastic corporal, the sole NCO in the party. At the end of a lengthy discussion, conducted upright in front of our slit trenches, this corporal put forward the party's views. They were alone, their guns had been destroyed and they had nowhere to go. Could they stay with us? From everyone's point of view, it seemed to be a sound arrangement. All of them had weapons, and none seemed to lack enthusiasm.

Calling Douglas over, I told him that he now had a fourth section in 7 Platoon, and within a few minutes the Poles were digging hard under the tutelage of their corporal, the only comprehensible part of whose name sounded like Peter. Huggins watched the work in silence. It was plain that he did not altogether approve of the new arrivals. They were not infantrymen but gunners, and foreign gunners at that. What was more, their fire control was somewhat sketchy.

The digging had hardly started when a jeep roared down the track from the direction of Battalion Headquarters. As it braked to a stop in the cover of the trees, Jimmy Gray jumped out and ran towards us.

Gray's news was startling. We were all to withdraw to Wolfhezen in fifteen minutes time. The Boche were pressing our other battalion so hard that the Brigade's vehicles were in danger of being cut off north of the railway line. Because of the need for speed, the Colonel had cancelled his previous orders, and the companies were now to pull straight back to the Wolfhezen level-crossing.

At first it was hard to believe that Gray had not made a mistake. Had he got his instructions muddled? The clamour of the battle to the north was getting steadily nearer, and the risk of our retreat being cut off was plain, but this was a suicidal way to withdraw. One could not just stand up and walk away from an enemy right on one's heels. In daylight the only way to withdraw was to move by bounds with platoons and companies covering one another back. Any other plan was madness. Things over in the north must be bad indeed for the Colonel to be rushed in this way. But Gray's instructions were unshakeable. Tired though he was, he seemed quite rational, fully recovered from the shock caused by the morning's slaughter.

I all but snatched the walkie-talkie from Huggins' hands. To my relief both 8 and 9 Platoons answered. The set was working. Sergeant Nesbitt had already seen the troops on his left preparing to move, and he sounded surprised, justifiably so, that he had not been told what was happening. As I was telling the two platoon commanders to bring their men back as quickly as they could, I noticed Robert Watson watching me. His face registered shocked disbelief.

Within five minutes, 8 and 9 Platoons had both arrived, followed closely by Battalion Headquarters. There was still little to be heard in front. Perhaps the Boche had not yet discovered that we were on the move; certainly both of our own forward platoons had slipped away through the trees without attracting the attention of the enemy.

David Unwin came next with some forty men of 'B' Company. He was now in charge of the pitiful remains of the company which had attacked through the woods only a few hours earlier, many of them bandaged, all exhausted. Impassive and self-contained, David's solid bulk towered over the men around him. He seemed untouched by the horrors of the day. Did I look like that myself, or was the strain starting to show on my face?

It would have been reassuring to have had a few words with David, to have discussed what was happening, something which neither of us could do with anyone else. But there was no time to do more than exchange a trite greeting as he passed.

Following the tail of a further party from Battalion Headquarters, the RSM in charge of them, I led the company out on to the track, down towards the open ground which we had crossed early that morning. It was the fourth time we had gone that way during the past twenty-four hours. Now the ground was littered with the hulks of gliders, some still smouldering, and the bodies of the Polish gunners. Bullets flew over our heads. A body of men from the other battalion was converging on us from the right. Then, about fifty yards in front, a man fell and lay still on the track. Now mortar bombs started to explode around the marching men. The pace quickened a little. A party of RASC appeared, moving in the same direction. The Colonel's jeep drove past, a sign that the whole of the Battalion must have got away; otherwise the Colonel would not have moved.

Telling Luke, who was by my side at the head of the company, to follow the RSM, I dropped back to watch how the platoons were moving. The pace was far too quick; some men were all but running to keep up. If this continued, the column was likely to split. It was reassuring to see the Poles moving well; now that things were going badly, they were showing that they were soldiers. I passed two men lying by the side of the track, one bandaging his leg with a field dressing, the second being cared for by a medical orderly.

But as I had expected, little by little cohesion was starting to break down. Some men of the mortar platoon had overtaken us, despite the weight of the loads, and were mixed up among us. There were two small groups from another unit in the middle of 7 Platoon. From somewhere in front – a long way off – a Spandau sent its bullets flying harmlessly overhead, but men were looking apprehensive and flinching. We were now under fire from two different directions. At any moment the Boche would find the range, and then the slaughter would begin. It was no longer an orderly retreat; the withdrawal was taking on the nature of a horde of men seeking safety. Soon discipline would crack and everyone would start to run.

I realized that I must get back to the head of the company where I could do more to control its speed of movement, but we were now covering the ground so quickly that it was impossible to overtake the platoons without running, and to do this could well start others off. I tried to contact Luke on the walkie-talkie, but the set was dead – probably batteries once again. Bullets now seemed to be coming from every direction except the safe left flank where we were protected by the steep railway embankment towering over us. Without stopping I turned my head to look back. Field-grey figures were debouching from the wood behind the Johanna Hoeve buildings. Tripping over a large stone, I wrenched an ankle, and was saved from falling only by Harrison's clutching hand.

What a target we must be! Some five hundred men from four or five different units, rapidly coalescing into a solid moving mass. What had happened to the German armour? There would be no sort of defence against SP guns roaring out of the woods on the tail of our disorganized troops.

The men ahead were stopping. Some were still pushing on but the voices of officers and NCOs could be heard cursing them into some sort of obedience. Half-a-dozen figures appeared on the top of the embankment, silhouetted for a moment against the sky before they leapt out of sight down the far side. A dozen or so others were clawing their way up the steep, bush-covered bank. One of them fell, clutching his stomach, and started to roll towards the bottom.

As I reached the front of the now stationary Company, the Colonel, with Gray and a couple of signallers, was standing by the side of the track. The dust-caked fatigue lines on the Colonel's face masked any emotion which he might have shown at the imminent destruction of his Battalion, and when he spoke his voice revealed no hint of anxiety. So far only a few men had been hit, but to continue like this across the open ground would be disastrous, he explained. We would therefore cross the embankment at this spot and find our own way to the rendezvous at Wolf-hezen in the cover of the woods on the other side. Meanwhile the vehicles were already driving as fast as they could towards the Wolfhezen level crossing.

The Colonel turned away to speak to the Adjutant who had just arrived with the rest of Battalion Headquarters. The last section of 'B' Company was disappearing up the side of the embankment. Seeing Luke a few yards ahead, anxious for his instructions, I called to him to follow 'B' Company and to wait for the rest of us on the other side. There was no sign of Watson or of Huggins. Either they had been hit or they were rounding up stragglers at the back. Nor could Douglas Thompson's 7 Platoon be seen. Gathered together in a group in a fold in the ground were Sergeant Nesbitt with 9 Platoon and CQMS Bower with company headquarters. Shouting to Bower to bring them all on behind me, I started up the bank.

Hauling myself up the steep cinder-blackened slope, clutching at bushes to check slipping feet, I noticed that the enemy fire had quickened. This was a little like clambering across the firing butts on the range in the middle of a machine-gun practice.

Down below, 8 Platoon, followed by some of Sergeant Nesbitt's men, were disappearing into the safety of the trees. I caught sight of the Colonel on my right darting across the rails in the middle of a jumble of men from Battalion Headquarters. Turning, I was relieved to see Robert gesticulating towards Huggins who was standing in the middle of a small bunch of men. Then a burst of Spandau fire ricocheted off the railway line, the bullets whistling over my head. On the heath below, a couple of mortar bombs exploded. This was not a place to linger. The sustained noise from behind suggested that the German armour was on our tails. Heaving myself up, I jumped for the slope, boots ploughing into the loose soil and cinders as if I were running down the side of a mountain.

We caught our breath in the wood. David's men had disappeared, and there was no sign of the Colonel or of Battalion Headquarters. No one had followed us. We were the last across, but a quick check told me that only Robert Watson, the CSM and three or four other men were missing, in addition to 7 Platoon. Of the latter there was nothing to be seen. In all there were still about fifty men with me, not counting Peter and his seven Poles, still clinging tenaciously to us.

Perhaps I should try to get back across the bullet-spattered embankment to find out what had happened to the others? But the noise of the battle was getting even louder. The Boche must be closing in. The vital thing must be to rejoin the rest of the Battalion with the fifty men I still had, and not to leave them in Luke Tyler's charge while I returned on what could only be a foolhardy errand. But it was difficult to avoid the thought that perhaps I was reluctant to climb back over the top of that embankment.

It was quiet now. For the first time that day we were in no immediate danger. Muffled by the trees and the railway embankment, the noise of the firing had receded into the background. After a few minutes in the woods, walking parallel with the embankment, we had emerged into a large open glade, broken up by a few copses of well-grown beech trees. Across the short grass the late afternoon sun elongated their shadows. For a moment there was contentment. One was still alive, and some order had returned to the day.

The mood was shattered no sooner than created. Sergeant Weiner's voice, harsh with excitement, jerked me back to reality. Scattered across the grass ahead were six parachute containers, each still attached to its vivid circle of coloured nylon. Some pilot, either in error or distress, had jettisoned his load out here, well away from the flight-path of the aircraft. Food and ammunition! I remembered hunger once again. Soon we must have food, if our strength was to hold out, but even more important was the need for ammunition. Three-quarters of the Bren magazines were empty; the spare bandoliers which many men had been carrying last night had all been used; and many of them were reduced to no more than twenty or thirty rounds each for their rifles. Only Sten gun magazines were still full and no grenades had yet been used: all the fighting had been at long range.

CQMS Bower, with Harrison and Jones helping him, was already opening the first container, his fingers fumbling in his haste to discover its contents. There was a curse of disappointment. It contained ammunition for the 6-pounder anti-tank guns, of no value to us at all. Sergeant Weiner, who was opening the next one some yards away, called across to say that the contents were the same. With Corporal Pritchard I ran to the third, and together we wrenched it open. Angry and disgusted, I swore obscenely. Then, remembering Pritchard's prejudices, I glanced rather shamefacedly in his

92

direction, to observe him doubled up in silent laughter. The irony penetrated and I laughed myself, rather too loudly. Crammed tightly in the container were serried rows of brand new red berets!

By now all the containers had been opened. The rest were full of the anti-tank ammunition. About a dozen men had gathered around the berets, swearing or laughing, before I swept them back to their sections with a reminder of the target they were offering any wandering Boche patrol.

Despite my disgust, I knew the explanation. The contents of supply-drops had to be pre-packed to a standard formula, and anything or everything might be wanted in the course of a battle – ammunition of a multitude of types, medical supplies, radio batteries, and even red berets. After all, the beret was a valuable psychological weapon. Ever since the airborne troops had first worn this new headdress in action in Tunisia, the enemy, both Boche and Italian, had learned to hate the sight of it. Everyone dropped with his beret tucked into a pocket, and little notice was taken when someone mislaid his weighty steel helmet. After all, the latter's value was limited: it might deflect a not too heavy fragment of shrapnel, but it would certainly not stop a bullet. Already quite a few men had rid themselves of their helmets and were wearing their berets – wearing them squarely on their heads in the airborne fashion as no one else could.

Probably only the one container of berets had been included in that supply drop, and it was just our luck to happen on it.

The laughter soon evaporated, leaving behind it a residue of disappointed exasperation to remind us of our hunger. The empty stomachs were my own fault. My annoyance with myself for ordering them all to load their packs on to the farm cart lingered, but what angered me even more was the fact that this error still nagged when there was so much more to occupy my mind than regrets for past blunders.

The noise of vehicles ahead interrupted this self-castigation. The first reaction was that they must be German, but the sight of a red-bereted figure walking towards us along the foot of the embankment set my mind at rest. It was Captain Mellon, the Brigade Intelligence Officer, a very old friend who had served with the Battalion since it was first raised, before being removed to the staff. A kind, gentle person, Mellon was not assertive enough to have made a good company commander, but his penetrating brain was an asset in his present work. Now his face was shining with pleasure as we approached; he could well have been greeting a collection of old friends met unexpectedly in Piccadilly.

Mellon had been put there to shepherd stray parties back to their units. 'B' Company, with the Colonel and Battalion Headquarters, and a number of the survivors of 'A' Company had already arrived, and were sorting themselves out about a couple of hundred yards ahead. A tunnel which no one knew about had been discovered under the embankment, and the noise which we could hear came from the Brigade's vehicles forcing their way through it. Now that a way had been found for the vehicles to cross, the Brigadier had decided to halt and collect the Brigade here, some two thousand yards short of Wolfhezen.

Stopping the men for a moment, I climbed to the top of the embankment with Mellon. Below, in a cloud of dust, a jeep towing a 6-pounder was revving its engine as it ploughed through the loose soil at the entrance to the tunnel, half-a-dozen men from Brigade Headquarters helping it forward with their shoulders. Supervising was the Brigadier himself, his small, spare figure vibrant with energy. In a wide half-circle around the tunnel entrance were scattered a number of other vehicles, including a couple more guns and an armoured carrier, waiting their turn to escape through the narrow concrete corridor, just wide enough to take a farm-cart, to the comparative safety of the far side of the embankment.

After the chaos of the past few hours, it was good to see the organized activity. Some of the men around the guns and jeeps looked nervous as they watched the vehicle being heaved towards the entrance, but there was no sign of panic. As yet the battle had not reached this point, but the sound of firing seemed to be closing in upon us in an ever-contracting arc. The gun and its jeep were through, and another was being signalled forward. At any moment the first burst of machine-gun fire would sweep across the flat open country. It was a race to get the transport through before the Boche arrived.

From our perch on top of the embankment the view was magnificent. The rolling farmland merged into the woods, their trees just touched with the first traces of autumn, the peace of the scene contrasting with the nearby din of battle and the sight of the struggling men below. I jerked myself back to life. No more than a couple of minutes had been wasted, but it was time that could ill be afforded. Turning towards one another, Dermot Mellon and I exchanged rather guilty smiles, aware of one another's thoughts. Side by side, without a word, we slithered down the steep embankment to the group of men below.

Ten minutes later, we found the remnants of the Battalion. Half of 'A' Company, the mortars and what was left of the machine-guns were missing, as well as our own 7 Platoon. More than one third of the men who had withdrawn from the woods around Johanna Hoeve had failed to cross the railway. We were now down to no more than a couple of hundred men. No wonder the Colonel had been so patently delighted by our arrival.

The day's peregrinations were not yet over. The Brigade had been ordered to leaguer for the night south of the railway embankment, and the place allocated to the Battalion was in the area where we had found the parachute containers. Back again through the woods we plodded, and then the entrenching tools were once more at work. Fortunately we were allowed to dig in peace. For some reason the Boche were granting a respite; the pursuit seemed to have been called off. Perhaps they too had been hit hard.

The sun had dropped behind the trees, taking with it what remained of the warmth of the day. A dank chill lay about the woods. By now the tea should have been brewed and the contents of the Compo packs warmed up, but for the second evening in succession there was nothing in our bellies.

At the end of my final tour of the company positions before the evening stand-to, I stopped for a word with Luke Tyler. Standing side by side in the failing light, we listened to the chink of metal against stone and the rustle of displaced sand as the men put the final touches to their trenches. High above us, a hundred yards away on the top of the embankment, four men on standing patrol were straining their ears and eyes for warning of the Germans. In the distance, from every point of the compass, the noise of the battle rumbled on.

I passed on to Tyler the news which the Colonel had given me thirty minutes before. Although it was now more than forty-eight hours since the first lift had landed, there was still no sign of relief. The rear-link radios at Division were not functioning, so no one had any idea what progress, if any, the 2nd Army were making. If help did not arrive to-morrow, the prospect would certainly be grim. The 1st Brigade at the bridge were said to be at their last gasp and incapable of hanging on much longer, and, after the disasters of the day, all hope of reaching them had been abandoned. The divisional troops, together with the remnants of the Airlanding Brigade had concentrated in a place called Oosterbeek, a small suburb of Arnhem about a couple of thousand yards to the east of our present position. Their southern flank rested on the river, so even if the Arnhem bridge was lost during the night, the 2nd Army would still have a bridgehead at which to cross the Rhine. Tomorrow at first light the Brigade would move into Oosterbeek to join the rest of the Division. But unless ammunition, together with air and artillery support, was forthcoming, the prospects were far from good. We were, it seemed, not opposed by a few third-line troops. Elements of three SS Panzer Divisions had been identified in the battle. The Germans seemed to have moved very quickly, or else something had gone wrong with the intelligence. It was not surprising that the day's fighting had been so very bitter.

In talking to CQMS Bower and Sergeant Nesbitt before I reached Tyler's platoon, I had done my best to be as cheerful as possible, but it was plain that the two NCOs realized that I was making the best of things. With Luke Tyler it was different. I could not insult him by trying to disguise our straits. I just told him the facts as I had received them from the Colonel. Possibly it was a mistake. Quite suddenly the failure of it all oppressed me. In less than thirty-six hours, two-thirds of the Battalion had gone. Fifteen rifle company officers had landed; only two were left; ten for certain had either been killed or wounded. The chances of surviving another day were small. Fatigue and hunger had drained me. There was a need to unburden myself. Luke was my junior in rank but equal in years, and in any case it was easier to confide in someone who was in many ways a stranger. Even as I spoke, I was ashamed of this weakness, but there was no stopping. Quietly Luke gave me the re-assurance I needed. The iron needed to sustain oneself through such a day was easily expended and I felt that I had purloined some of Luke's share.

CHAPTER FOUR

DESTRUCTION

I CROUCHED in the slit trench, my Sten gun pointing over the muddy parapet, still stiff with the night chill, despite the early morning walk around the company area. The second night had been even worse than the first. Two days growth of beard itched my chin, and my teeth needed cleaning. Wet trousers clung to my legs. My left hip ached from lying on my water-bottle when snatching an hour's sleep just before dawn, but at least my right side was unbruised. The pistol was no longer there; I had given it to Lance-Corporal Williams the night before. Somehow the company clerk had been separated from his rifle during the withdrawal and had arrived weaponless at the night bivouac.

It was quiet now, half an hour after stand-to. I could even hear the drops of water blowing from the trees to spatter the fallen leaves below.

The night had been a misery in every way. At irregular intervals from the late evening onwards, clusters of mortar bombs had fallen among and around us, harming no one but preventing sleep, at least for me. Others, between spells of sentry duty, had collapsed exhausted into oblivion. Four times enemy patrols had roused them from their stupor as the night exploded into noise and light, with red tracer whipping the trees and white flares blossoming overhead.

No one had been hit, but losses there had been. On stand-to rounds I had found the Polish trenches empty except for Peter, their corporal, crouched grimly behind his Bren. The rest of the party had vanished in the early hours, sensing perhaps that they had attached themselves to an unlucky unit. Peter explained nothing, but his embarrassment was clear; it was both unfair and pointless to press him for details when either pride or sense of duty had kept him there to fight on among strangers.

The thought of what would have happened if the enemy had attacked from this direction against a position held by the one solitary man was chilling. It was a mistake to trust strangers. I had learned yet another lesson: rely only on those you knew.

I glanced at the men drawn up by the side of the track, ready to move off towards Oosterbeek. Dirty, weary and famished though they were, they still managed to look like soldiers, their weapons clean and equipment neat, chinstraps fastened and berets on straight. Perhaps Oosterbeek might provide them with food and shelter, and also a little rest. That is, if they ever got there.

To reach Oosterbeek, we were to make a wide circle through the woods. David, with 'B' Company, was to lead along the usual sort of sandy track which at first drew us away from our final destination. Next came Battalion Headquarters, and last 'C' Company, now once again a sizeable force, the Colonel having sent us the remnants of 'A' Company to replace the missing 7 Platoon. In charge was Kelly, their own sergeant-major, a small, square taciturn Glaswegian, as hard as the paving stones of the Gorbals alley where he had collected the razor scar which all but cut his nose in two.

After some ten minutes, 'B' Company turned to the left and disappeared out of sight. This would be the junction with the Breede Laan, which from the map led down to the main Arnhem–Utrecht road at a point about half a mile to the west of the outskirts of Oosterbeek. It was quiet among the beeches, the only sound the swish of boots rustling the fallen autumn leaves. To the east, the noise of guns, muffled by the trees, was now no more than an unminded accompaniment.

I turned into the Breede Laan. Running slightly uphill, the avenue cut a pencil-straight line through the woods, the branches of the beech trees which lined its sides meeting overhead in a solid green canopy. So little of the early morning light penetrated the arched tunnel that I could barely see the men ahead, hugging the sides of the track in the wet gloom. Disturbed by all this unusual activity, a red squirrel darted across the carriageway to scurry into the branches where it watched us with quizzical interest.

Eyes soon adjusted to the light. Ahead, at the top of the rise, the sky was now visible under the archway of trees. For a moment, two or three men were outlined on the crest before they disappeared down the road. More followed. Then, as I had feared, the quiet of the morning was swept away by the harsh cacophony of enemy machine-guns. A couple of men collapsed on the skyline and lay in a heap in the middle of the road. Ricochets whined in the branches above us. The column stopped, men dropping into the ditches which bordered the road or sliding for shelter among the trees. In a moment only three or four men were still to be seen, standing in a knot at one side of the track, just below the crest. The Colonel was one. David must be among the others. Soon some thirty men crossed to vanish in the woods on the left. Minutes later, the sound of Spandaus and Brens spread over towards the direction where these men

101

had disappeared. The noise, now intense, ebbed to swell again. Then for some ten minutes there was near silence before the din erupted once more.

It was obvious what had happened. David's leading platoon had been stopped by enemy lying in wait on the reverse slope of the hill; the rest of 'B' Company had then tried to find a way around the left but had also hit the enemy. The Boche seemed to be everywhere.

After some fifteen minutes, the anticipated summons crackled over the radio. Sunray (that incongruous codename for all commanders, whatever their rank) was to report straightaway to Battalion Headquarters.

In the early morning light, the Colonel seemed to sag, his youthful fire all gone. Oosterbeek had promised to be a refuge for what was left of his Battalion. Now the way was blocked once more.

The Colonel described what had happened. It was as I had guessed. About a hundred yards away, over the crest in front, the Germans were in strength, and 'B' Company could make no progress among the houses and trees on the left. Now the Colonel wanted 'C' Company to attack around the right to secure the junction where the Breede Laan met the main Utrecht road.

Rapidly I passed on the orders to Tyler, Nesbitt and Kelly, who had moved up behind me while the Colonel had been talking. From where the four of us lay at the top of the crest, a few yards off the track, the slope fell away steeply below towards the main road. Among the dense trees, there were glimpses of roofs of largish houses. Of the Boche there was no sign at all, but anything might be waiting for us down there in that tangle of houses and gardens. Without being able to see where we were going, the only thing to do was to probe forward with one platoon ahead and the other two following, one behind the other.

8 Platoon led the way. Two of its sections were in front, moving side by side through the trees, with Luke Tyler and his runner in the middle giving direction. Close behind, I followed with Private Harrison, just to the rear of Luke's reserve section, Sergeant Weiner's. The rest of company headquarters was some fifty yards back, followed in turn by CSM Kelly's platoon and Sergeant Nesbitt's.

Nothing happened for the first hundred yards. A few rounds from the direction of 'B' Company whistled through the trees overhead. Then Luke's leading men crossed a narrow road and were among the gardens and the drives of the plush suburban houses perched on the steep hillside. I followed Weiner down one of the drives which took us around the corner of a square white-walled house, from which well-groomed lawns and formal flower beds dropped in tiers to the road below. Opposite, on the far side of this road, the ground rose steeply once again in a manner un-typically Dutch. On this further side of the valley, no more than a hundred yards away, we could see scattered houses and gardens similar to those through which we were picking our way.

Already we were quite close to our objective. The circle was half complete. Once we reached the road, we would be able to take the enemy positions on the Breede Laan in the rear. From now on we would be able to see where we were going, and so could advance on a broader front.

I sent Harrison away at the double to direct Sergeant Nesbitt down the drive of the next door house, from which his men could drop on to the road parallel with 8 Platoon. Ahead, I could see that Weiner had halted to cover the advance of the two leading sections of his Platoon which had begun to edge their way gingerly down the slope.

103

The firing started with a single Spandau. Then a second joined in, to be followed by the whistle and explosion of mortar bombs falling all the way along the slope. I darted across to a clump of bushes. Half across them lay the body of a lance-corporal; it was one of Luke's men, but the face was hidden. As I threw myself down, a single shot sang past my head. Then a long burst of bullets hit the body beside me, half turning it over on to its back. Not waiting to find out who it was, I squirmed on my stomach for some fifteen feet before daring to peer out to discover what was happening. From the garden of the house immediately opposite, a gun-flash all but coincided with the familiar Spandau rattle and the clatter of bullets striking the house wall to the left. Another burst and windows shattered. Weiner's Bren and rifles were firing back. Two bombs burst behind me. The Bren stopped, but the rifles went on firing.

There must be at least half a dozen Spandaus on the other side of the valley, as well as a couple of heavy machine-guns. There was not the slightest chance of our clambering down across those lawns with such numbers of Boche shooting at us from less than a hundred yards away, and even if we did manage to reach the road, we would be no better off.

Some twenty feet away, Luke Tyler was beckoning me, half-sheltered by the side of the house. Steeling my nerves like a shy girl entering a crowded room, I sprang for the protection of the wall, zig-zagging twice as I ran. There was a door. Luke was through it, holding it open for me.

We were in a sitting room, a neat place, some sort of study with a desk and some etchings on the wall. There were no windows other than the glass garden door through which we had entered.

I needed to catch my breath before speaking. Then, safe for the moment within the shelter of the house, we exchanged news. One of Luke's sections was pinned down among the lawns, but he had managed to pull the other back to the far side of the house.

He was explaining what he had seen of Sergeant Nesbitt when the room exploded about us in a searing crash. Both of us were flung to the ground by the shock-wave from some object which seemed to pass level with my eyes. Covered with plaster-dust and rubble, I lay for the moment, blinded, dazed and deafened, before I could force open my eyes and drag myself to my feet. Peering through the white dust-cloud, I saw that the wall on the German side had been pierced at eye level by a circular hole about twelve inches across. In the wall opposite was a corresponding gap. A round of solid anti-tank shot had entered one end of the room, passing within a foot of our heads as we talked.

The Germans had seen us both enter the house and had tried to winkle us out with an anti-tank gun. They would not be content with the one shot. Seizing the still dazed Luke by the shoulder, I dragged him through the now glassless door into the open air. As we flung ourselves to the ground, there was another crash and another dust cloud rolled out of the door.

It took us a couple of minutes to recover. Then, as Tyler turned to make his way back to see what he could do to extricate his section pinned down in the garden, his plaster-white face broadened into a smile, grim but sardonic, deprecating the bloodiness of it all.

Walking back down the drive to find Sergeant Nesbitt, it struck me once again that Luke's men were fortunate in their officer. Although 8 Platoon had done everything asked of it, its casualties had been far less than those of the others. There could be a measure of luck in this, but the way Luke's men had fought was not altogether due to chance. This quiet, rather elderly subaltern, still almost a stranger, could take most of the credit.

105

Harrison and Kelly were approaching from the other end of the drive. Although Harrison had left only forty-five minutes before, it seemed more like a couple of hours, so much had happened. I had become so accustomed to having Harrison nearby that I was uneasy when he was not there. An extension of myself was missing, another pair of eyes and ears, another hand with a Sten in it. But more important still, it was a relief to see him back unharmed. One had come to expect bad news.

And once again, it was bad news. Sergeant Nesbitt's platoon had been trapped on the slope leading down to the road, in the same way as 8 Platoon's leading section, but far more men had become embroiled. Nesbitt himself was badly hurt, shot through the thigh, and had been dragged into a house, where Harrison had seen Corporal Pritchard splinting and bandaging him. At least four other men had been killed or wounded, while several were missing. CSM Kelly, seeing what was happening from the rear, had managed to extricate the survivors and bring them back to join his own platoon in the trees behind.

The sound of a vehicle from the road below interrupted Kelly. Then there was the noise of another, together with the beat of a couple of Brens and the explosion of a small mortar bomb. With Kelly and Harrison following, I dashed back along the drive to the damaged house where I had parted from Luke, and peered with caution down the hillside. Slewed across the road was some sort of small German truck, a field-grey figure slumped across the steering wheel; in the road a second man was crawling painfully towards the shelter of the garden opposite, one leg dragging inertly in the dirt. Fifty yards further on, another and larger truck lay overturned and burning, its bonnet crushed into twisted metal against the trunk of a large tree. Nothing moved near it. Then, from the direction of Wolfhezen, I could hear

106

another engine labouring up the hill, and around the bend an armoured half-track gingerly exposed itself, two rows of steel-helmeted figures crouched along the benches at the back. From below, Luke's two Brens again opened fire, and an explosion in the middle of the road indicated that the 2-inch mortar had found the range. As the half-track accelerated up the road to vanish out of sight, tracer was bouncing off its armoured flank and two sprawling bodies were half hanging out of the back.

So intent on the road had I been that I had failed to notice that the Germans in the houses opposite were again shooting. Mortar bombs were bursting all over the place, and some sort of gun was firing as well, possibly an 88 mm; it could have been the one which nearly killed us in the house, but now it was using high explosive at point-blank range, traversing across the gardens in front. Only the one Bren was now replying, together with a few rifles, all from the direction of Sergeant Weiner's rear position. I ducked as a sustained stream of Spandau bullets shrilled overhead.

We were in a mess. The Boche on the other side of the valley outnumbered and outgunned us. There was not the slightest hope of reaching the back of the Breede Laan this way, and to stay here, on this forward slope, was impossible; at this rate we would soon all be dead or wounded. Somehow I had to get the survivors back up the hill, but it was a near insuperable problem with the men scattered down there among the houses, lawns and shrubberies, shot at every time they moved.

Someone called from the side of the house. As I turned to look, Private Gregory darted across to throw himself down beside me. Under the dirt and two days' scrub of beard, his face was a greyish white; he seemed about to vomit.

As Gregory stammered out his platoon commander's name, I knew what had happened. Lieutenant Tyler was dead. I could think of nothing but our talk the evening

107

before. So my self-centred premonition had been wrong. Luke was dead, not me. Not, at any rate, for the time being.

It must have happened just after we parted. Luke had been killed on the steep garden path which led from the house down to the road. He had been hit by a sniper, killed outright by a bullet through the heart within a couple of yards of the place where Gregory was lying. Possibly Luke had been careless because he was still dazed, but he had to get back to his platoon, and the path was the only route.

This was how officers and NCOs were killed, just doing their routine job. This was why casualties among the leaders were so high. All the time they were moving about, checking here, encouraging there, backwards and forwards. Now, besides myself, only CQMS Bower and Sergeant Weiner were left. All the rest of the officers and sergeants in the company had gone.

One problem, however, had been solved. The remnants of Tyler's two forward sections had managed to extricate themselves, without waiting for orders. Since last night Private Gregory had been in charge of one of the sections, both the NCOs having been hit the day before. During that last mortar stonk, a bomb had fallen right on top of the corporal who was commanding the other section, blowing both him and his Bren gunner half to pieces. Common sense had told the survivors to quit, and there had been no one to stop them except Gregory, who for the moment was shaken by the sight of what had happened to his friends, and who in any case lacked the authority to hold them there. No one else had been hit in the scramble back, and the survivors were now sheltering in the house.

The position we were now holding was far from orthodox, but it would have to serve for the time being, although it

108

broke every rule in the book except that it provided an excellent field of fire. We were lying in a straight line along this path, shooting into the belt of trees, some two hundred yards away at the bottom of the slope, where the enemy were hiding. On the left was the large water-tower which had helped us keep direction as we retreated up the hill, but now it would provide a useful ranging mark for the Boche. The massive row of beeches running along the side of the path marked the exact extent of our position along the top of the ridge. Already the camouflaged figures had made a half-hearted attempt to advance up the slope towards us; a couple of humped shapes showed where they had been stopped. There was no one in reserve, and the Boche had been so close on our heels that we had not had the chance of scraping any holes for shelter.

I had not been able to make an exact count, but there must be about fifty men left, including Kelly's reinforcements. They were now organized into two platoons, with CSM Kelly on the left and Sergeant Weiner on the right; in the centre were the half-dozen or so members of company headquarters. The rest of the Battalion should be no more than about a hundred and fifty yards behind, but close though they were, we had heard nothing from them. The radio, which had been faint enough when we started, had failed to work as soon as we left the Breede Laan. Colour-Sergeant Bower had gone across to find the Colonel and report what had happened to us, but as yet he had not returned, nor had anyone from Battalion Headquarters come to look for us. There was no means of telling what was happening, although in the woods over towards Oosterbeek the rumble of battle swelled and broke, never stopping, varying only in pitch and volume.

I hated it here, stretched out in this long straight line, but until some instructions arrived it was better to leave the men where they were. The enemy fire had slackened for the time being. Probably they were deciding on their next move. If they brought up their 88s, they would blast us off the top of the ridge in a couple of minutes.

The others were as uneasy as I was. For the first time I was unhappy about them. Until now they had endured the successive disasters, but the events of the morning had tried them too far. It had been yesterday once again, yet another failure against an enemy who was far too strong for us. Men were looking jittery; some could well be near breaking point.

As I gazed down the slope, trying to spot some activity among the Boche, a movement to the right caught my eye. About twenty yards away, two of Kelly's men were moving diagonally behind me, sheltered on the far side of the ridge. My shout made them hesitate, and then stop after two or three more steps. Forgetting the enemy, I stood up and strode down towards them. No explanation was necessary, the surly guilt on their faces was enough. Deliberately, choosing the words for effect, I cursed them in language rarely used by officers towards soldiers. It was enough. The two men turned back towards their platoon.

Worming my way back to the top of the ridge, I found one of Weiner's Bren gunners. The man had slipped behind a large beech tree into a position which sheltered him from the enemy fire, but did not allow him to use his weapon. Seeing his company commander so close, he slid back into his firing position, fingers white against the trigger guard.

In this mood the men would never stand up to an enemy attack. Even a mortar stonk could break them. I could see it happening. First one or two men would slip away, like the two I had just stopped, and then a rush would follow. Something drastic had to be done.

No more than the occasional rifle bullet was now coming over. In fact, no one had been hit since we took up our position along this ridge. It seemed safe enough.

Standing up, I began to walk along the path towards the left of our position. For the first few steps I felt wretchedly vulnerable, but then an odd exhilaration seized me. Not too slowly and not too quickly, I strode deliberately towards the first group of men. Grinning down at Lance-Corporal Williams, I made some inept remark about it being the wrong place for a company clerk.

If I were to be hit, it would happen anyway. Now seemed to be as good a time as ever.

Stopping at each group of men, I checked their firing positions and made changes as necessary. Then I was at the end of Kelly's line of men, and I started back, conscious that everyone was watching. There was a burst of machine-gun fire, well wide of us, but I managed to avoid flinching at it.

Suddenly Sergeant Weiner's voice, harsh with concern, was yelling at me to get down, demanding angrily what I was playing at. The spell broke. I was grateful for the excuse to lower myself down beside him, very relieved that it was over. The rage in Weiner's face dissolved into an un-accustomed grin.

The corny dramatics were over, but they had served their purpose. The men had again got a grip on themselves, but the effect would soon wear off, like a hot cup of tea drunk half-way through a freezing night. A mug of tea then would, in fact, have had much the same effect on them.

A rifle bullet thudded into the tree trunk about three feet above my head. Again I was glad of Weiner's intervention. For the past five minutes that sniper must have been busy elsewhere. Private Gregory's Bren stuttered twice in response to the bullet, and then stopped with a single shot. Gregory answered Weiner's testy query. The Bren magazines were all empty.

Wriggling back off the top of the ridge, I walked behind it down to Kelly. It was as I feared. Kelly had only four full magazines left for his three guns, and the riflemen averaged no more than ten rounds each. The morning's fighting had been costly in ammunition. The men might have regained the spirit to fight, but now they lacked the means to do so.

Ammunition we must have, and we needed to find out what was happening. Wrong though it was to leave the company at such a time, I would have to visit Battalion Headquarters myself. Ammunition would be in short supply, if there was any at all, and I was likely to have to argue for it. In any case I must explain our parlous state to the Colonel. Kelly would have to look after things for a bit, but he should be all right; certainly he had proved his steadiness that morning.

It took Harrison and myself less than three minutes to find Battalion Headquarters, still where we had left it a couple of hours before, around the junction between the Breede Laan and the track coming in from the east. From the noise, 'B' Company was still in action over on the right. Two sprawled figures lying alongside a burnt-out jeep were an additional reminder that the headquarters had also been involved in the battle. Under a tree by the side of the lane, where the Medical Officer had set up his Aid Post, lay a dozen wounded men, some bandaged and wrapped in blankets, others waiting attention, their torn uniforms showing the stained dressings covering their wounds. The Doctor, morphia syringe in hand, rose to his feet from a stretcher on which lay a man face downward, his back swathed in dressings. Bare-headed and shirt-sleeved, his arms bloody to the elbow, a weary smile creased the Doctor's face when he saw who it was, but he turned without a word to the next body in the row, too preoccupied for pleasantries. He was a genial and active man, always thought to be more

112

interested in parachuting and weapon-training than the practice of his profession. It had been something of a stale joke that the Doctor would be a better man to have in a tight corner than attending to one's wounds. How wrong we had been.

The Colonel was glad to see me. There had come to be both surprise and pleasure in each meeting now. Only seven officers were left, together with some ninety men still capable of fighting. David Unwin was among the seven; I had hardly dared to venture the enquiry, but the Colonel anticipated my question.

It was clear why we had heard nothing from Battalion Headquarters for the past two hours. Like everyone else, the signallers, orderlies and clerks had been fighting for their own survival. The Germans were all round them, and had been pressing hard throughout the morning. Now, the Colonel told me, the Brigadier had decided to try a thrust in a fresh direction, after this failure along the line of the Breede Laan. The other battalion was to take the lead, striking due east, directly towards Oosterbeek. Behind would follow the brigade troops, while we were to bring up the rear.

After the Colonel had explained how we were to withdraw when the time came to do so, I put the question about ammunition. There was still a small reserve left, it was a relief to discover.

Conscious of having been away for too long, I hurried off in the direction of the ammunition jeep, but could find no trace of it. In turn, we asked three or four men for directions, but no one could help. Time was speeding by. I was eager to get back, and a rattle of fire from the area where we had left the company increased my worry. Then, at last, I saw the person I wanted. Sitting next to a jeep, his legs stretched out in front of him, was the RSM, the man responsible for the ammunition reserves, apparently at ease. The warrant officer looked up at us, but made no move to get to his feet.

My regard for the RSM was high; I both liked and admired him, feelings which I always hoped were reciprocated. But here the RSM was in the middle of the battle, sitting on his arse and taking his ease, while a company commander hunted for ammunition. Majors are not in the habit of rebuking RSMs, but this was too much. The tensions of the morning had snapped my self-restraint, and in a couple of succinct sentences I told the RSM what I thought of him.

Then the RSM apologized, but he did not move. Without any trace of irony or annoyance in his voice, he quietly explained that he could not stand up because he had been shot through both legs. I had not noticed the airborne smock with which someone had covered his outstretched and bandaged legs.

There was little to be said. The RSM did his best to reduce the embarrassment, but with little success. Nor was there any time to waste. Harrison and I leaned over into the back of the jeep, grasped a rope handle each, and heaved out the solid wooden box with its precious contents of a thousand rounds of ·303 ammunition. Carrying it between us, we turned to go. There was nothing to be done for the RSM. We could only leave him there to be picked up by the Germans in due course with the rest of the wounded. Relieved to get away, we said good-bye and wished him luck.

Although we had been away for no more than twenty minutes, it was a relief to find the remnants of the company still where we had left them. We were only just in time with the ammunition. The Germans had attacked again, another rather half-hearted effort, but in stopping them the last few rounds had been fired from the Brens. The box we had brought was enough to fill thirty magazines, and the men were soon busy at the fiddling task, forcing the rounds down with their thumbs, placing each with its rim just so as to avoid the disaster of a weapon jamming. Meanwhile, Harrison, with Williams to help him, had returned to the jeep for a further box. For the present, everything seemed to be quiet, although from the woods over towards Oosterbeek floated a steady rumble of noise, suggesting that the other battalion was in trouble trying to force the fresh route towards the rest of the Division. One thing was quite clear. Our sole hope of survival was to reach Oosterbeek. We would not last much longer out here in the woods.

Harrison and Williams arrived with a second box of ammunition. It had been the last in the jeep, but as there was no one about they had decided to remove it and get away as quickly as possible. Of the RSM there was no sign; probably he had been moved to join the rest of the wounded with the Doctor.

On the way back, a sniper had fired a couple of rounds at them as they crossed the track, but otherwise their journey had been uneventful.

It was another half-hour before Jimmy Gray brought the order to move back to the Breede Laan where the Battalion was to concentrate, ready to try the easterly route into Oosterbeek. It was the old Jimmy once again, his nerve fully recovered. What reserves of strength the man had! Many were near breaking point. It could happen to anyone at any time, but few were fortunate enough to recover in the way Jimmy had done.

Every instruction seemed to arrive by word of mouth, usually Jimmy's. So much for radios. It was a little like Waterloo, with gallopers rushing about the battlefield, carrying orders from one wing to another.

After another unexplained delay, we started at 1 o'clock, moving not down the track towards Oosterbeek, the way

115

the other battalion had gone, but plunging to the left of it into the woods, here quite open, the copses of well-grown trees broken up by clearings, some newly planted with waist-high saplings. Of the ninety men left, about half were members of 'C' Company. No one seemed quite certain where they were going or what was happening. It was all so hopeless. Out here in the woods, we hardly stood a chance.

Only too soon our fears were justified. A Spandau opening up ahead sent us all to the ground, men diving for cover just a little too quickly. A moment later, a second gun fired on us from the right, but it was the ominous rattle of the tracked vehicles which chilled – first one, then another, then two more, quite close and in front, their engine clatter rising above the din of the machine-guns and the rifles. Then, about seventy yards away, I saw the first of the SP guns, its stubby weapon traversing slowly towards us. The flash from its snout was one with the explosion of the bursting shell. Just to the right, a half-grown tree shattered into jagged splinters. A second shot, following hard on the first, covered Harrison and me with earth. We were swamped by the noise. Every sort of weapon seemed to be firing; grenades were exploding, but distinct above the rest was the clank and the throaty cough of the armoured guns. Caught like this in the open, we were helpless. Tanks ploughing about among us could have been no worse. There was no way of fighting back; no one seemed to have even a Piat, and we could not get close enough to use the Gammon bombs, the bags of plastic explosive carried for use against armour.

Then the guns veered to the left, and in a few seconds they had gone, as suddenly as they had appeared. The men in front were moving forward again. I stood up, signalling to those behind to follow. We were doubling now, but there was still some sort of control. We were not running away, but making for somewhere. Where, I did not know. Some

116

tennis courts ahead, surrounded by high wire netting, forced us to swing to the right. Two dead Germans lay by the side of the wire. Then we were crouching in shallow ditches on either side of one of the many lanes which intersected the woods in every direction.

Somehow or other, we seemed to be mixed up with Brigade Headquarters. In a clearing about forty yards away, three jeeps were parked, all marked with the Brigade number, and all with trailers. Two of the jeeps stood close to one another, and on one of the trailers a wounded man lay motionless on top of the load. The tall figure of the Brigade Major walked across from the group of vehicles, but he had nothing to tell us except to suggest that we stay where we were for the time being. He mentioned that the man on the trailer was a badly wounded lieutenant-colonel, some liaison officer.

Leaving CSM Kelly in charge, I went to find out what lay on our left. Quite near, only about fifty yards up the lane, I discovered the Colonel, surrounded by a handful of men from his headquarters, together with a few stragglers from other units who had gathered around him. The only officer was Jimmy Gray. From the Colonel I learned that Dermot Mellon had just been killed, trying to find his way back to Brigade Headquarters. I remembered our meeting on the railway embankment the evening before and allowed recollections of the past to obtrude into the harsh present.

For the moment the battle had swept beyond us, but the noise of it was still there. Soon the enemy would find us again.

There was a sudden burst of fire from the left as I was working my way back down the lane. An answer was tapped out from the direction of the Colonel's party. Scuttle-helmeted figures darted through the trees. Two of them fell. Again there was the clank of the tracks, and the snub snout

117

of the SP gun was peering at us over the top of a bush. Three times it fired. At the third shot, the jeep next to the one on whose trailer lay the wounded lieutenant-colonel burst into flames. As if content with its work, the armoured gun drove off through the trees towards the corner where I had just left the Colonel. Again the gun coughed three times.

I had thrown myself into the ditch next to Sergeant Weiner just as the shell hit the jeep. At first the flames spread slowly, but soon they were clawing out towards the trailer with the wounded man. A driver, who had been sheltering near it, stood up and ran towards us shouting a warning that one of the vehicles was loaded with ammunition. All of us watched, fascinated by the inevitability of it all, waiting for the explosion, no one móving. Perhaps it would be better for the ammunition to explode; then the officer would die quickly, not burn slowly to death! Although there was nothing to be done, guilt nagged me. The figure on the trailer never moved. Perhaps after all the man was unconscious.

Then, out of the clump of trees on the right, a short, spare figure was running across the grass towards the burning vehicle. It was the Brigadier! Springing into the driving seat of the jeep attached to the trailer on which lay the wounded officer, he seemed to be shielding his face from the flames which shot from the vehicle next to it. Then the engine roared into life, and with wheels spinning in a cloud of sand, the jeep and trailer roared across the clearing as he threw out the clutch and rammed the throttle to the floorboards.

Glancing along the line of soldiers crouched in the shallow ditch, some of them huddled behind the moss-green trunks of the beech-trees, I wondered how close we now were to being finished. It seemed incredible that the Brigadier had not been hit, with the volume of fire which was sweeping the clearing. Perhaps the Boche were shooting badly? Was it

118

possible that they were shaky as well. But then, about a hundred yards away, I caught a glimpse through the trees of a German half-track. It stopped and helmeted shapes jumped from its sides. How many more of them were there? This could be the start of another attack, which could only end it all. Our will to fight back was all but broken.

From a bunch of trees about thirty yards to my left, someone called my name. It was the Brigadier's voice. For the moment, the enemy fire had slackened. Gingerly, I worked my way towards the place from which the voice had come, finishing with a short dash across an open stretch of ground.

The Brigadier was not lying down, but standing upright behind a bush which might just have concealed him from the enemy. It was necessary to stand, because from ground level we could see no more than the bushes a few yards ahead, but we were very exposed. I found the Brigadier's apparent unawareness of the danger intensely irritating, still more so when we moved a few yards to the left to get a better view. Here a dozen young trees provided no more than an apology for protection against the bullets, but we were able to obtain a clear view of a clump of trees, about a hundred and fifty yards away, some of which seemed to be growing out of a number of small bumps in the ground. It was some sort of hollow, the Brigadier said, where a large party of Boche had gathered. The flash of a Spandau from under one of the trees confirmed the statement. Then I heard the Brigadier telling me to clear the enemy out of the hollow, after which the survivors of the Brigade would join us there. 'C' Company, it seemed, was the last organized body of troops left.

For a moment I was so dumbfounded that I hardly heard the Brigadier going on to say that the Brigade Major was dead as well, killed about five minutes ago. Another friend

119

was gone, but I hardly listened. What was the Brigadier ordering us to do in his quiet and determined fashion? It was absurd. The men were finished. Only a few minutes ago I had realized that they were past defending themselves. Now we were being told to assault that Boche position.

The Brigadier's look was both quizzical and encouraging. The confounded man could see what was passing through my mind. Then I was away, dodging back through the bushes towards the men in the ditch, even more aware than before of the bullets singing overhead.

With my back to a broad tree which hid me from the enemy in front, I looked down at the upturned faces. There was no point at all in wasting time on details. The orders I had to give them were quite simple, devoid of any complications such as who would provide covering fire. It was a time for play-acting again. My naturally loud voice carrying down the line of men above the sounds of the battle, I bawled at them to follow me, adding the comment that it was better to be killed going for the bastards than lying in that bloody ditch.

No one hesitated. The men rose to their feet the moment I stepped out into the open from behind the shelter of the tree. Glancing to my right I was exhilarated by the sight of David Unwin's solid bulk running parallel with me, half-a-dozen of his men following. David shouted something to the effect that they were coming as well, and I waved my Sten gun in acknowledgement. Behind me Sergeant Weiner broke into a scream of rage, harsh and furious. The yell spread down the line. Too heavily laden and too tired to sprint, we lumbered forward towards the enemy in a sort of jog-trot. Now I was careless of everything. We did not stand a chance, but this was the right way to go. This was the proper way to finish it all. Nearly hysterical now with rage and excitement, I heard my own voice join in the screaming.

120

The Germans were shooting at us. I could see the flashes of their weapons springing out of the gloom of the trees. There was no need to look back to confirm that the line of men was still following. The noise told me they were there.

Now the Boche were no more than fifty yards away. As I brought my Sten down to hip level to press the trigger, it flashed through my mind that it was the first time I had fired the weapon since the battle started. My forefinger squeezed the metal. Nothing happened. It had jammed. Here I was, running towards the enemy with a useless piece of metal in my hands!

Our feet made no noise on the soft carpet of fallen leaves across which we ran. Silhouetted against the sky, the beech trees reared up ahead from among the mounds where the enemy lay. Between their stems, a patch of green meadow, vivid in its contrast to the muted tones of autumn, showed in the distance. There were figures moving among the trees. First a couple, then half-a-dozen dark shapes were outlined against the green background, men sprinting away, men disappearing through the trees. The Boche were running away.

We had done it! We had driven the enemy out at the point of the bayonet! This was the ultimate in war!

The sight of the savage, screaming parachutists streaming towards them had been too much for the Germans, even though they had to do no more than keep their heads and shoot straight.

From the lip of the hollow, I looked around, savouring the moment. On the right, someone flung himself down on a bank to open fire with a Bren at the last of the enemy who were vanishing across the green pasture towards the shelter of the trees on the far side. Five paces away, a German soldier, his young features lined with pain and fatigue, gazed up in horror, wondering how long he had to live. Beside the man was a Mauser rifle. I snatched it up, checking quickly that there was a round in the breech, before I flung away the Sten, glad to be rid of the useless gun.

The sight of David on the right added to my delight. Shouting to him to hold the right of the hollow, I directed Sergeant Weiner round to the left. There was no need to tell anyone to hurry. They all knew that the Germans would not delay in mounting a counter-attack.

A moan of terror distracted me. I turned to the wounded German. The man's features were contorted into a rictus of despair. Above him stood CSM Kelly, red-eyed and panting, his bayonet raised above the soldier's stomach. But Kelly did not strike. He was relishing the moment, snatching the maximum of pleasure from the wounded man's anguish before he sliced into the soft belly.

As my newly-found Mauser knocked the bayonet to one side, the sergeant-major snarled at me in unspoken protest at such silly scruples. Then he seemed to shake himself. The blood-lust passed away, and he came to his senses, gathering his men together to man the defences.

The Brigadier was there, generous in his congratulations, giving orders for the defence of the hollow, the whole of which was now in our hands. Everyone was elated by the success, slight though it was. After being chased around these woods by the Boche for the past two days, at last we had struck back and seen the enemy run. We were ourselves again, ready to fight, different altogether from the dispirited wretches who half an hour ago had crouched for shelter in that ditch. Something had been snatched back from the disasters of the day.

The remnants of Brigade Headquarters, together with a few stragglers from other units, had now arrived. In all, there seemed to be about 150 men with half-a-dozen officers. As well as the Brigadier, David and myself, there was

122

Jimmy Gray. The latter brought news that the Colonel was probably dead, although he could not be sure as they had become separated during a scrimmage with an SP gun. Of the rest of the officers who had jumped with the Battalion, Captain John Simmonds, the gunner FOO, was the only one left.

The hollow was not a single feature, but a number of holes, some as much as fifteen feet deep. They had the appearance of being large bomb craters, in places so close together that they were separated from one another only by steep, high banks, but they were probably old excavations of some sort. The branches of the trees growing from the top of these banks, which we had seen silhouetted against the sky as we had advanced, met overhead in a canopy, through which only stray flickers of sunlight were able to penetrate. Carpeted in a deep, soft bed of leaves, it was a dank, grim place, some fifty yards wide and a hundred or so from end to end. Along the Oosterbeek side there ran yet another of the myriad lanes which intersected the woods, with a fence beyond bordering the bright green field across which the enemy had run away. Because this open field could be covered so well from the line of the fence, the Brigadier had included the latter in the defensive position. As a result we were holding a piece of ground of about a couple of acres, a compact area, just about the right size for 150 men, not crammed too closely together and not too far apart from one another.

It was only just after 2 o'clock. So much had happened during the past hour. Around me some men were checking and cleaning their weapons, while others were hacking furiously into the sides of the banks, using either entrenching tools or scraping away with their bare hands. Some men were hunting for discarded enemy weapons. In one of the hollows, seven or eight German wounded were being

123

searched for ammunition. As I stuffed a hundred rounds of Mauser ammunition into my pouches, I tasted the unaccustomed harshness of a German cigarette, one of a packet which the accomplished Private Jones had just lifted from the corpse of its erstwhile owner. Everyone was busy. Someone was in charge. We knew what had to be done. So long as the Boche did not produce tanks, we would be able to hold this place. Of that, I was sure. But we had little or nothing with which to defend ourselves against enemy armour.

The first long stream of Spandau bullets to whistle through the trees and ricochet around us was answered immediately by a steady succession of bursts from a Bren gun. Soon the sound of firing encompassed the perimeter. I crawled to the top of the bank to join Harrison, just in time to spot a camouflaged figure dart from a clump of trees and drop behind an isolated bush about forty yards away. Lifting my new rifle to my shoulder, I fired three carefully aimed rounds in rapid succession into the middle of the bush. Nothing moved. I pulled my binoculars out of the front of my smock and levelled them on the target. To the right of it, where the leaves were more sparse, a hard, still outline was visible. I fired again, another steady shot, but the shape did not move. I was sure that I was not missing at that range, even with a strange weapon.

After about fifteen minutes, a lull in the shooting suggested that I might now be able to get round and visit the Battalion positions. The Battalion! For the first time it struck me that I was now in command of what was left of it. Pitiful remnants, but they were still fighting!

The Brigadier had allotted the south and west sides of the perimeter to us. The first pit held Sergeant Weiner with seven or eight men. At the bottom, his eyes shut, lay a grey-faced and motionless Private Gregory, shot through the stomach.

124

Corporal Pritchard had bandaged him and given him a shot of morphia, but because his airborne smock had been pulled down over the blood-stained dressing to keep him as warm as possible, he lay there with no outward sign of injury, looking as a man might do who had collapsed with exhaustion.

Gregory's eyes opened. When he saw who was standing over him, he asked for the favour. His voice was quiet, his words measured and coherent, his proposal quite logical. Out here, without the help of a doctor, he was going to die in any case, and he could stand the pain no longer. Would someone please put a bullet through his head?

For the moment my grip tightened around the Mauser. In Gregory's state I would probably be asking for the same release; if it did happen, I hoped that someone would have the guts to give it to me. Then I caught Weiner's eye, and he knew that I could not do it.

The only way to help Gregory was to give him a further shot of morphia, dangerous though it would be to do so. As I reached for my own ampoule in the breast pocket of my smock, I was ashamed by my reluctance. The reason was purely selfish. Sooner or later I might want to use it on myself, wounded and alone behind a bush with no one about to help me. But Sergeant Weiner came to the rescue. He had scrounged a supply of ampoules from somewhere or other. Opening the small black tin, he bared Gregory's arm, and pressed the needle home.

The words of sympathy and encouragement sounded pitifully trite as I pressed Gregory's shoulder. Nervous of any reproach which I might see, I turned and walked away without looking the wounded man in the face.

The clatter of tracks, followed by the thud of a gun from the direction where the German had died behind the bush, sent me clambering back to the vantage point on the lip of the adjacent hollow. Again the gun fired, splintering the tree above my head. Just in front a man was propelling himself along the ground on his back, a Piat clutched to his stomach, sheltered by a slight fold in the ground. It was a strange NCO from another unit, moving with the speed and economy of movement of an instructor in weapon-training demonstrating a field-craft lesson. The man reached the tree for which he was making, about sixty yards from the armoured gun and sideways on to it. Bringing the Piat slowly into his shoulder and lingering on the aim, he fired. The projectile exploded squarely on the vehicle, somewhere around the engine, but it did not catch fire. Only two members of the crew jumped for safety on the far side of it, to scramble away in the shelter of the trees. The gun was silent.

The NCO seemed to be in a hurry to regain the shelter of the hollow. Rejecting caution now that the gun was out of action, he jumped to his feet and sprinted towards the place where he had left his comrades. The Spandau burst hit him full in the back when he was almost there, hurling him towards the bottom of the bank where he lay in a motionless, crumpled heap.

I ducked as a bullet whistled past my head. So intent had I been on watching the poor devil with the Piat that I had grown careless. I had been exposing myself for far too long on the edge of the hollow. Moving a few yards to the left, I pushed my head up once again and looked around. Other than the smashed gun, there was no sign of any other armour. Why did the Boche not produce a few tanks and finally finish us off? Two or three Piats could do little against a proper armoured attack, and everything would be over in a few minutes. As it was, the only immediate worry was the dwindling stock of ammunition. Crammed into so small an area with the enemy all around us, it was almost impossible for the Boche artillery and mortars to hit us

126

without harming their own troops. The odd mortar bomb fell among the hollows, or exploded in the branches overhead, raining jagged metal fragments around our heads, but otherwise the battle had settled down into an intermittent exchange of rifle and machine-gun fire, swelling now on one side of the perimeter, now on another. It was perilous to raise one's head or move about for fear of the well-placed German snipers, but there was no sign of the enemy making any further attempts to try to get to grips with us.

It must be clear to the Boche that the opposition was tough. They would gain nothing by wasting men on fruitless attacks, when all they had to do was to wait for us to run out of ammunition or for some tanks to turn up.

Time was dragging a little. For the first time since we woke that morning, there was a moment to spare. Again there was a consciousness of minor inconveniences. I had not eaten for forty-eight hours. Shoulders had been rubbed by equipment, and the wounded hand, forgotten except when I had to grasp the stock of a weapon or dig, had again begun to throb. Although my water-bottle was half full, I could not allow myself the indulgence of the gulps needed properly to quench a nagging thirst; there was no knowing when it could be refilled, and in any case its contents might soon be needed for the wounded, now numbering a dozen or so, for whom Corporal Pritchard was doing his best.

My name was being called. It was Private Jones, slithering towards me down the opposite slope of the hollow. Jones told me quickly. It was Major Unwin, killed by a sniper, shot through the forehead as he was peering over the rim of the hollow, trying to locate the whereabouts of a Spandau. He had died instantly. Jones was adamant: there was no doubt at all that he was dead; his brains had been blown out.

Jones was urging me to come and see his body, but I could not bring myself to do so.

127

But David could not be dead. They could not have killed David. Everyone else, yes. One after another friends had died, but I had never believed that this could happen to David, so vast, so indestructible, the humorous, gentle David.

The Brigadier was beside me. He also had heard the news. For nearly two years he had known us both, and it was plain that he understood the anguish. But there were other things to think about. The Boche fire had cleared some of CSM Kelly's men out of their positions along the fence on the Oosterbeek side. Whitehouse, the orderly-room sergeant, who had been fighting all day as a section commander, had been holding the fence with a few odds and ends from Battalion Headquarters and elsewhere. A machine-gun, firing from the far side of the green field, had killed him and a couple of his men, and the survivors had been withdrawn across the road to the lesser danger of the hollow. Poor Whitehouse! He should have been in England, making out his returns, but he had pulled the many strings he controlled to secure a seat for himself in the Colonel's aircraft.

The Brigadier had sent for the rest of the few surviving officers and senior NCOs. Now we were gathered in a circle on the ground around him.

As we knew only too well, the Brigadier told us, our ammunition was nearly finished, and as our own fire slackened, the enemy snipers were becoming bolder and more men were being hit. Soon we would be forced to surrender, so he had decided to take the initiative. We would break out towards Oosterbeek, charging through the enemy in a solid mass, trusting to our numbers and impetus to get us through.

It was an extraordinary pian. For the second time that day the Brigadier was ordering us to do what seemed to be impossible. But our trust in the Brigadier's judgement was now implicit. It was a gamble, but one which offered at least a chance of success. To stay here could only end one way.

Fifteen minutes later, we were ready, something more than one hundred men crammed together on the Oosterbeek side of the position, facing the lane where Whitehouse had been killed. The rest of the hollow was deserted except for the German prisoners and the wounded, three of whom had insisted that they would come as well when the Brigadier and myself had gone over to say good-bye to them. It was some slight consolation to be leaving the rest of the wounded to an enemy who could be expected to care for them properly.

By making a detour, I had managed to avoid passing the place where David lay.

There was now no time to waste. We must be away before the Boche sensed what we were doing.

It could have been the start of a race. The Brigadier asked whether we were ready. Then, at his shout, the hundred of us rose to our feet and exploded in a solid mass over the lip of the hollow. In front was the Brigadier himself, leading the way. Behind came the yelling, screaming men, filthy and blood-stained, weapons in their hands, bayonets dull and menacing, a fearful sight to anyone in our path.

The remnants of the Battalion were at the rear, with myself leading them and Jimmy Gray at the back. Somewhere in the middle ran CSM Kelly.

As we crossed the lane, someone was shooting at us from an arched wooden gateway on the left. By the side of the gate lay a wounded German, shot through both legs, silent, his face imploring us not to kill him. Just ahead was another one, dead, a flame-thrower strapped to his back, the ground in front of him blackened. It was the first of these weapons which I had seen in the battle. Wondering how it was that

I had not heard before that the enemy were using them, I was thankful for having been left in ignorance.

The German fire now seemed to be coming from every direction, but I saw no one hit. We were rushing downhill, along a lane, a solid human battering-ram.

The first wild pace slackened; the firing had stopped. We had done it! We were through the enemy and out of the forest! For the second time that day boldness had saved us.

Ahead were some suburban houses. We had been running for rather more than a quarter of a mile, and now we fell into a shambling walk, catching our breath, an untidy mob of men making for safety, not a formed military body. Just outside the houses one could see the parapets of slit trenches with camouflaged helmets showing above the line of soil. Still, the Brigadier led us on, so they must be ours. The sight of a couple of red berets quelled all doubts. Now I was level with the trenches, carefully dug, trim and tidy. It was the Border Regiment, an airlanding battalion, the men just as trim and tidy as their trenches, but businesslike as well, a world removed from the gang of haggard, filthy ragamuffins who followed me. Some of them stopped without permission asking for cigarettes or water, so I decided to call a halt for the moment. Still half-hysterical from their exploit, they started to tell their tale.

It was too much for the young captain of the Border Regiment in charge of the position. He was a forceful man, no respecter of rank. In a few well-chosen words, he suggested that the filthy shower should be removed before they contaminated his troops.

I should have been annoyed, but could sympathize with the captain, who had been confronted with what was clearly an undisciplined mob, hammering down the lane, running away from the Boche towards the shelter of Oosterbeek. There was nothing to suggest that these men had fought their way all day through the woods against armour and flame-throwers, to finish with an overwhelmingly successsful assault against the enemy who had surrounded them. There was no point in explaining matters, and in any case our tale could hardly improve the morale of the listeners, even if they believed it. Rather in the manner of a commissionaire mustering a cinema queue, I moved the men on, to the further disgust of the captain.

Someone was leading us into the garden of a large house. The men dropped to the ground as they halted, conscious now that they were safe, with houses and other British troops around them. Others, after a swig from a water-bottle, lay supine, unconscious in instant sleep.

I counted them. Jimmy Gray, John Simmonds and Sergeant Weiner were there. CSM Kelly was missing; some-one had seen him fall in the rush. There were just forty-nine other men, about half from 'C' Company. Last night there had been two hundred. The night before, five hundred. More than three days had passed since the 1st Brigade landed last Sunday. The 2nd Army was now thirty hours overdue.

THE BATTALION IN OOSTERBEEK

Major Tom Angus
Lieutenant & Quartermaster Hugh Elkins
CQMS Bower
Pte Harrison
Corporal Galbraith
Pte Jackson
Corporal Pritchard
L/Cpl Williams

1 Platoon
Captain John Simmonds, R.A.
Corporal Day (MT)
Pte Oswold (QM's Storeman)

2 Platoon
Captain Jimmy Gray
Sgt Weiner
Pte Jones
Pte Robertson

CHAPTER FIVE

DEFENCE

FROM the first-floor window of the solid detached house standing at the corner of the road, I looked across towards the park, staid with suburban herbaceous borders and carefully tended trees. In the garden below, sunflowers dropped over faded summer roses and clumps of Michaelmas daisies.

The owners of the house must have left in a hurry the previous evening, just before Jimmy Gray's platoon had arrived. Their half-eaten meal strewn across the dining-room table had augmented the sparse tins of Compo ration, while the cellars had produced enough gigantic bottles of preserved fruit to give each of the twenty-five men a plateful as relish to his second mug of tea.

We all had quite a different look about us this morning. Although I had been able to snatch no more than about three hours sleep between midnight and dawn, broken into two interrupted spells, most of the others had managed a good night's rest. Their bellies held something again, not much, but enough to revive them. The night under a roof, wrapped in a Dutch eiderdown, or perhaps a floor-rug, with more tea and a cigarette to clean their mouths on awakening, had made the world seem a different sort of place.

Also their pouches and bandoliers were full. The jeep which had brought the food from Div HQ had pulled a trailer loaded with several sorts of grenade, ammunition and spare weapons. I had divided the fifty men into two platoons: one was made up of the survivors of 'C' Company, with Jimmy Gray in charge; the second included everyone else under John Simmonds, the gunner. There were now enough weapons to equip each platoon properly with three Brens, a Piat and a small 2-inch mortar, together with a Spandau or two which had been acquired in the hollow.

The speedy way these supplies had arrived had been heartening, suggesting that the people at Div HQ were properly organized, and that some reserves of food and equipment did exist, however small they might be. Our own headquarters was even linked to Division by field telephone. So far everything had been quiet, but if we had to fight in these houses, we were ready to do so. It had been a transformation. Now we looked as workmanlike as the neat airlanding troops of the previous evening, not the ragged survivors of a military disaster.

But I hoped that the end was in sight. Last night, in the cellars of the Hartenstein Hotel, just before dark, the General, now returned to the fold, had told me what to do. It was less than an hour after we had reached Oosterbeek.

Other than those few men who might still be fighting at the Arnhem bridge, the survivors of the Division had been collected in this prosperous little town, a sort of Dutch Esher, with something of Cheltenham about it – all comfortable commuters and retired colonial officials from the East Indies. The part held by the British was pitifully small, no more than a mile deep and three-quarters of a mile wide, the southern flank resting against the river. Earlier that day, the Americans had seized the bridge over the Waal at Nijmegen, so with all the obstacles behind them crossed, there was no reason why the 2nd Army should not arrive within twenty-four hours.

As was to be expected, the General's attitude was one of rugged optimism, but in my own mind was the doubt that the 1st Parachute Brigade would be able to hang on for much longer at the bridge. The men there had been told to defend it for forty-eight hours, but they had now been fighting for nearly four days, and no help of any sort had reached them. The end must be near. But if the 1st Brigade were to be wiped out, this bridgehead at Oosterbeek was another possible crossing place for the troops of the 2nd Army.

The General told me that there was a gap in the north-east corner of the perimeter which the survivors of the Battalion were to fill, in between some airlanding troops on the left and some other men of our own Brigade on the right. On the General's map the small rectangle of streets which we were to hold appeared to be only about 150 yards long and some fifty feet deep. We had discussed the problem for a minute or two, and the General suggested that we might do best by using our small force to hold the houses at the two corners of the diagonal.

After the chaos of the woods, it had been oddly calm and orderly down in those cellars. The marked maps which we had been consulting were pinned neatly to the walls. In the room opposite, a couple of staff officers pored over lists and message forms, while a haggard radio operator at the end of the passage muttered hopeless incantations into a mute but still crackling set. It was hard to remember that the Germans were only about a quarter of a mile away.

As I walked away from the graceful three-storied building, the last vestiges of daylight had revealed wide lawns dotted with fine cedars and beech trees. The spoliation of war was somewhere, but in the half-darkness I could barely see the trenches, the shell-holes, the shattered branches, the wheel-ruts in the lawn, and the graves topped with rough wooden crosses by the corner of an outbuilding. Until I reached the

135

tennis courts, there had been little sign of life except for a passing orderly and a sentry or two. Then suddenly I realized that the area behind the high wire fence was crammed with men. I stopped, puzzled, listening to the hum of talk and wondering at the crowded, humped figures, scattered on the ground. Private Harrison was the first to notice that they were not speaking English. The men were Germans. The tennis courts were being used as a prisoner-of-war cage and were crammed with Boche prisoners, an oddly alien presence in what otherwise could have been the familiar wartime surroundings of a country house requisitioned for the troops. It was all so peaceful after what had happened during the day. Over to the east, the rumble of guns was a reminder that the 1st Brigade was still fighting at the bridge. Only an occasional burst of firing echoed back from the outskirts of Oosterbeek. Had the enemy also had enough for the day?

After seeing Gray's men into place in the house overlooking the park, I had returned to spend the rest of the night at my headquarters, which was placed with Simmond's platoon at the rear of the diagonal. The telephone line back to Division lessened our isolation, but it had kept me busy during the hours before midnight. Staff officers wanted to know this or that, or to tell me something or other, most of it inconsequential. At last I had fallen asleep, to be woken again by a false alarm after an hour or so. Then I was wanted again on the telephone. And so it went on, but for all that it had been a quiet night. At least the enemy had not bothered us, and the snatched spells of sleep had cleared my brain.

Now I was back again with Gray's platoon, and the sun was coming up above the trees across the road. Private

Jones, who was acting as runner to Jimmy, had brought mugs of tea as we arrived, slipping them into our hands with a conspiratorial grin. I had come up in the dark, before stand-to, troubled by the isolation of this forward platoon. The area to be held had looked quite small on the General's map, but here in the streets it was different. Neither of the two platoons could support the other, their fields of fire confined by the houses, hedges and trees.

There was a lot to be done. We had arrived last night in the dark, weary and cautious of moving about in the strange streets, wary of bumping into either the enemy or our own side, both of whom could be equally dangerous. Nevertheless, it was surprising to discover that Gray had made no contact with the units on either flank. Nor had trenches been dug, other than a couple in the garden for sentries, but this was more understandable. Trenches dug in the dark would give shelter, but little more; only in daylight could one be sure that they had a proper field of fire. Probably Jimmy was nearer to utter exhaustion than I had realized, more weary even than I was. It was a further reminder that men of around thirty tended to have greater stamina than the young.

The beat of a couple of Brens, mixed with the familiar sound of Spandaus interrupted these thoughts. The firing came from the left. Possibly the Spandaus had our own troops behind them; so many captured weapons were now being used. Then, with the explosion of mortar bombs and the louder crash of artillery shells, the noise merged into a near solid roar. It was clear now what was happening. The Boche were attacking the airlanding troops who must be holding that group of two or three large houses about a hundred yards further up the road towards the station.

Just below in the garden, but out of sight, another Bren opened up. It was Jimmy Gray's sentry at the garden gate. There was a glimpse of a camouflaged figure running through

137

the trees opposite, no more than a hundred yards away, diagonally across our front towards the airlanding troops. Then a couple more. Jimmy's Bren fired again, and one of the figures pitched forward, rolling over, carried on by its own momentum. Further crouching men flashed through the trees. It looked as if the Boche had still to learn that we were holding this corner house. There was little doubt that they soon would.

Only then did it occur to me that I was watching a battle through a raised open window, intact sheets of glass hanging over my head. A bullet or a bomb splinter through the glass would slash my face into rags of flesh.

It took only a moment to smash the glass out of the frame with the stock of my rifle. We would have to fight from the house itself, not from the trenches in the garden. It was a sturdy building with thick, solid walls, and in any case the garden was too small for the purpose. From these upper windows we would have the extra range and observation to fire diagonally down the road in front of the houses held by the units to right and left.

Fifteen minutes later, the trim Dutch house had been wrecked. Every pane of glass had been smashed, and every picture and mirror knocked from the walls; there was no time to be careful. In the centre of each room barricades had been built, well back from the windows out of sight of the Boche, but sited so that every scrap of ground outside was covered. Sideboards and chests-of-drawers, stuffed with books or bedding, made the barricades, the contents of the furniture flung in heaps into the corners of the rooms. Mattresses were rolled down to the basement, ready for use, if needed, by wounded men. More books, crammed into drawers, were blocking those windows not required for shooting through. Fortunately, the owner of the house possessed a fine library; from its contents it seemed that he was a doctor.

With Gray, I walked around the house for a final check before leaving to return to my own headquarters at the rear. Manic vandals might have swept through it, some woman's life work ruined in the time it took to drink a cup of coffee. Books were important to me, to handle and to look at, as well as to read. The wrecking of the library had been particularly unpleasant.

In a single crammed week among the bomb-wrecked streets of Battersea, we had learned the theory of fighting among houses. It was something which the British army had thought little about until the war was nearing its end. There were no streets in the desert, any more than there were in the jungles of Malaya or Burma, and there had been little fighting inside the towns and cities of Italy and Sicily. We had first practiced 'C' Company in the skills of street-fighting in Jerash, the ruined Roman city set in the soft green hills above the Jordan, working from the notes of some half-remembered lecture, and teasing out the problems as we went along, defending and attacking in turn the little shops and houses in the single narrow street which still remained. Here, a couple of thousand years before, wine and girls had been sold to other foreign soldiers. The spring sunshine had warmed the old stones, and the war was a very long way off.

Then, back in England, we had fired our weapons, thrown grenades, and exploded charges among the pathetic, shattered, working-class houses of Battersea, cautioned to do no more damage than necessary so that a few precious walls and roofs were left for the string of units which were to follow us. Even in 1944, smashed streets were harder to come by than farmland for training soldiers. Jerash, Battersea and Arnhem! It was an incongruous combination, but I was grateful for that week in South London. At least we knew the theory.

Again a Bren fired, this time from the large front bedroom which I had just left. The noise drummed through the house, amplified by the constricting walls. A second gun joined the first, firing from the ground floor sitting-room which I was about to enter. I pushed open the door. Behind a sideboard in the middle of the room, lying on its side and packed tightly with oriental rugs and embroidered table-cloths, lay little Private Robertson, his cheek pressed into the butt of his gun. Robertson again squeezed the trigger. The din was deafening, the fumes from the muzzle acrid. I inserted myself into the space between Robertson and a thin, lanky youth who was pumping bullets with steady concentration through the empty window frame. In the park on the far side of the road, two grey-green mounds lay about fifty yards away, still by the bole of a tree. Another figure was dragging itself in frenzied, painful jerks towards the shelter of a tree-trunk.

A single bullet slapped into the wall behind, releasing a small cloud of plaster dust. A second was followed by a burst from a machine-gun, the bullets bouncing from one wall to another. The gun fired again. Sharp flakes of plaster, torn from the walls and ceiling by the ricocheting bullets, spat around us. A dense white pall of dust enveloped everything, blinding and choking. Yet another burst ripped half the window frame out. Harrison, lying on the floor behind me, cursed. Knuckles to his eyes, Robertson fell back from the Bren, blood running down his forehead, and was pushed aside by Sergeant Weiner, who seized the gun and fired two long bursts through the murk into the trees outside.

Slowly the dust settled. One thing at least was certain. The Boche knew now that we were in the house. I looked around. Harrison, his face white with dust, was examining his right hand, covered with red-stained plaster, from which blood dripped in a steady stream on to the floor. Someone was wiping the dust and blood from Robertson's eyes. Thank God the man could see. Weiner clicked the empty magazine off his Bren, replaced it with a full one and fired another long burst through the window. An explosion from above, followed by the clatter of tiles falling off the roof, drowned the noise from the gun. Another bomb burst in the garden, just outside the window, sending a couple of fragments whistling into the room. Now the Boche were hitting us with mortars as well.

Then it was quiet again. Quiet here, at any rate. On either side, the din of the battle, still resounded, while from further away in the streets behind, where the rest of the Battalion lay, came the noise of heavy firing.

Jimmy was in the room saying that upstairs two other men had been wounded, one by a bullet through the shoulder, a clean flesh puncture which had missed the bone. The other, like Robertson, had been hit in the face by splinters, but he was not badly hurt either. Both were in the cellar, and someone was now leading Harrison and Robertson down to join them.

I walked upstairs to examine the damage. Over everything, including the men's faces, lay a white coating of plaster, but it was a relief to find them all so cool and confident once again. Some were cleaning the clinging dust from their weapons and magazines, others watching the park and the houses on either side from behind their barricades. There was a comfortable sense of security in this solid house. Now it was our turn to sit tight and hit the enemy floundering about in the open.

It was so still that I heard the click of the latch on the front garden gate. Wondering, I slid along the wall towards the window so that I could peer down into the garden. Up the path was walking a small, elderly civilian, dapper and brisk in a smart brown overcoat and soft hat. He walked like a man in his own garden, unaware of the familiar surroundings, his mind on other matters. Perhaps he was short-sighted, maybe deaf as well, for he noticed nothing until he reached the front-door steps. Then he stopped, his face incredulous. Possibly he had heard or noticed us inside the house. Certainly he could now see the damage inflicted upon his home. Last night he and his family must have left in a hurry; the abandoned meal was evidence of the haste. Perhaps they had spent the night nearby with friends, but this morning, with the obstinacy of the elderly, he had insisted on returning, either to recover some valuables or just to reassure himself. He must have been very deaf.

For the moment the little Dutchman gazed in horror at the wreck of his home, the empty casements, the books spilling out of the windows into the garden mud, the shattered roof, and the filthy soldiers gazing at him from the murk of smashed furniture. With a single, strangled cry of misery, he turned and ran, clumsy and stumbling, out of the garden gate and up the road.

On the stairs I met Sergeant Weiner and told him about the man. There was no sympathy from that quarter. Among the books in the dining room, Weiner had noticed some works of Nazi propaganda, together with what looked like a membership certificate for a Quisling organization. Perhaps the man had received his due!

Five minutes after the Dutchman had disappeared, the mortar bombs again started to drop up and down the road. One fell in the garden, two more on the roof, smashing more tiles but hurting no one. Then something bigger joined in, the whistle of the approaching shells and the size of the explosions suggesting field artillery of quite a large calibre.

In the cellar five men were either lying on the mattresses or leaning against the wall, none of them badly hurt it was a relief to discover. Robertson was not among them. Whatever

142

had hit his forehead had inflicted no more than a deep scratch, and he was now back with his Bren, a strip torn from a white linen pillow-case around his head, his eyes sponged clean of blood and dust. With deft fingers, surprisingly gentle, Jimmy Gray had bandaged them all, giving Harrison and the man with the shoulder wound a shot of morphia. Slumped against the wall, both looked badly shocked. Another shell fell outside. The empty jars and bottles on the dusty shelves tinkled as the tremor shook the house from its foundations upwards. All of us flinched, wounded and unwounded alike, and did so again as another shell fell just up the road.

Harrison's wound was superficial, although he could not move his left hand. No bones seemed to be broken, but the pain had been intense until the morphia brought relief. He had little to say. For the moment he only wanted to be left alone.

As I mounted the cellar steps, I knew that I was going to miss Harrison's presence. Always by my side, anticipating my every movement, always ready to relieve me of minor chores, Harrison allowed me to conserve the last scant reserves of strength for the job in hand. I had lost nearly everyone now; without Harrison one would be that more alone. Both silent men, we had talked little, but the bond was tight. We had been together for a long time.

It was strange how inactive the Germans were. Their losses during the early part of the morning must have been heavy, and now they were wary about the occupants of these houses. Somewhere among the trees opposite, they were probably digging in, but they were not showing themselves. Only once in the past hour had a stream of Spandau bullets again filled the room with choking dust and flying splinters, but two or three snipers were ensconced out there as well, shooting at anything which moved. Already the lanky boy in Robertson's section had been shot through the bicep when he ventured too close to the window. Robertson, however, had got the sniper, firing back at the muzzle, flashing out of the gloom of the trees.

A shell exploded among the trees, about a hundred yards ahead, much larger than anything so far seen, sending a pillar of dust and smoke into the sky, and raining earth and stones into the road. My heart sank. This was medium artillery, large stuff. A hit by one of these would remove not just a few tiles, but half the house. Another whistled overhead to explode well into the enemy lines, followed by a third which fell about three hundred yards away, sending up a column of smoke among the trees where the Boche must be digging their trenches. My spirits rose a little. They were shelling their own troops. Soon, however, they would discover their error. Again the whine, this time louder, the noise of several shells. In the park opposite, one after another, half-a-dozen exploded. There was a short lull, and then the same happened again, the shells whistling directly overhead.

Now I understood. They were British guns, not Boche. Those first three rounds had been ranging shots, directed by some FOO with the airlanding troops next door. Then they had fired for effect into the park. They were medium guns, much heavier than the light weapons of our own airborne artillery regiment, so they must be from the 2nd Army on the other side of the river. At last there was some help from outside. The 2nd Army guns were within range. Soon we should be seeing their tanks and infantry as well.

No longer were we alone. Around me rose the chatter, shrill and excited. All day, whenever they had a few minutes to spare, the men had been mocking the sloth of the 2nd Army, the grumbles not the good-natured complaints flung

144

as a matter of course at other units and formations, but harsh scorn for troops who had let them down. The Americans had captured all the other bridges; they had done their job. The 2nd Army had only to motor up the road from Nijmegen. But at last something was happening. The relieving troops had shown that they were close at hand. Perhaps, after all, we might now escape from this trap.

In the middle of the afternoon, the Boche attacked the houses on either side of us once again, leaving us alone. For a time there was very heavy firing in and around the area held by the airlanding troops, but then it died down and all was quiet again. On the right, two parties of Germans crossed the road in a rush; two were shot as they ran. For about an hour the sound of further firing echoed backwards and forwards across the gardens, before it too faded away.

To our front the Boche snipers were still busy. Then, from directly behind us a Spandau opened up, shooting into one of the small bedrooms which overlooked the back garden. Were we isolated now, stuck out here by ourselves? Had the troops to the flanks pulled back or been wiped out? For the time being I kept these doubts to myself, but it seemed certain that the Boche had surrounded us. Were they now waiting to finish off the job under the cover of darkness?

The fate of John Simmonds and the rest of the Battalion was also worrying me. From time to time during the day, I had been distracted by the sounds of fighting in the streets behind. Every minute now I was becoming more and more anxious to discover what had happened to them, reproaching myself for having been trapped here all day with Gray's platoon.

A bullet splintered the empty frame behind me and buried itself in the ceiling, a warning that I was far too close to the back bedroom window. There was now a sniper behind us, as well as the Spandau. A quick movement in the garden of the house opposite caught my eye; then two figures in the wrong sort of camouflage darted from behind a bush into the shelter of a wall. They were Boche, not British. So the enemy were indeed all around us. There was no doubt now. I would have to stay here until it was dark.

Then the mortaring started again, not ranging up and down the street, but concentrating on the house. A direct hit into the slit trench by the garden gate, luckily empty, was followed by two more bombs exploding on the roof. Next, half-a-dozen dropped in succession into the road outside, sending a few splinters through the windows, but harming no one. Except for a sentry in each room, watching the park and the roads outside for any sign of an enemy attack, men pressed themselves into the floorboards, or crouched huddled on the staircase, well protected by the thick walls. It would take a large number of direct hits from mortar bombs to destroy this massive 19th century house, but each explosion still brought its involuntary shudder, hard to control. The cumulative effects of the past four days were starting to tell. I was wondering how much longer I could keep a hold on myself, when the mortaring stopped. It had lasted all of forty-five minutes.

Standing in the shadow of the house, we formed up in single file by the back door, for the time being sheltered from the glare of the flaming building a hundred yards away. As well as Private Jones and myself, there were six wounded men, none of them seriously hurt. Two, in fact, could use their weapons, but all needed to see a doctor and were more of a liability than an asset to Jimmy Gray. Jones was there as an escort, so that there would be at least one other fit man in the party. This left Gray with seventeen men, just enough to cover all the approaches to the house.

It was unpleasant to leave the seventeen men there, all except Jimmy survivors of 'C' Company, but our orders were to hold this corner. The fact that the troops on either side had disappeared, whatever the reason might be, was no excuse for withdrawing. For all that, I felt guilty to be leaving the men in this way, but there was no alternative. I had to discover what had happened to John Simmonds' platoon, and in any case I wanted to obtain permission to withdraw from this isolated corner. I just hoped that they would understand.

For the first fifty yards we moved in line down the narrow street, keeping close to the waist-high hedge, and stopping every fifteen paces or so to look and to listen. Except for some fitful shooting away off towards Div HQ, all was quiet. Then as we reached a junction and crossed to the other side of the road, the crunch of heavy boots into gravel broke the silence. There was no need to say anything. In one movement everyone dropped to the ground. From my haunches, I peered back down the file of men. At the end knelt Private Jones, Sten gun to his shoulder, aiming back the way we had come.

I raised my head over the garden wall which here bordered the road to see, less than thirty feet away, a line of German soldiers moving down the drive of the house which we had just passed, their helmeted heads and camouflaged shoulders visible over the hedge. There were ten of them. It only needed one man to glance to his left to see Jones crouched at the corner.

The patrol was a perfect target. With the advantage of surprise, we should be able to kill most of them at this range. Slipping back the safety catch on my rifle, I un-buttoned my left pouch and pulled out a Mills grenade, its

147

oval pineapple fitting neatly into the palm of my hand. I slid the index finger of my left hand into the ring of the safety pin, ready to pull. Still the Boche had not seen us.

I paused. The risk was small, but six of us were wounded, four quite useless in a fight. Any Boche who survived our first onslaught would probably hit back with the strength of despair, and there were certainly others nearby who could come to their aid. The important thing was to get these wounded men back, and then sort out the rest of the Battalion, not take needless risks which would have little effect on the outcome of the battle. My job was to hang on to this corner of the perimeter. Anything else was of little consequence.

It was too late. The opportunity had slipped by, and there was no longer any decision to make. The Germans were out of the gate and moving up the road towards the house we had just left. A minute's difference in time either way and the two parties would have met in the road head on.

When the seven men stood up to follow me down the road, I could see the relief in their faces. They, certainly, thought that I had done the right thing.

John Simmonds and his men were in the houses where they had been left that morning. Their delight at our appearance was understandable. Harrison and myself had been given up for lost when we failed to return from our early morning expedition, while they had been equally despondent about the fate of Gray's platoon. The absence of any news, coupled with the day-long sound of the harsh fighting on the edge of the park, seemed evidence enough that the forward platoon had been overrun and destroyed.

This rear platoon had spent much the same sort of day as the front one, except that the Boche back here had been rather less aggressive. John had made strong-points out of a couple of houses, smaller but just as robust as the one held by Gray. About seventy yards away on their left, they had discovered a party from the Recce Squadron under a couple of captains, old acquaintances both of them. The two groups had been working closely together, largely, I felt certain, because of John's charm of manner and determination. This young gunner had done very well. It hardly seemed possible that most of his men hardly knew him by sight yesterday. Today he had welded the survivors of four different companies of a unit of another arm into a tight entity, well capable of carrying on the fight. All day they had held firm, killing and wounding quite a lot of the enemy, but losing only one man themselves, a corporal of 'A' Company whose hand had been blown half off by a flying mortar splinter. Lined and filthy though his face was, eyes red-rimmed and chin stained with three days' growth of fair, fuzzy down, John still moved briskly, a reminder to all of us that we could still keep going.

Waiting outside the General's office, Harrison lay slumped asleep against the wall, his legs drawn up to avoid tripping the staff officers and signallers who moved backwards and forwards along the cellar passage. When the rest of the wounded were led away towards the dressing station, Harrison had declined to go. He could use his weapon after a fashion, he had protested, and he was certainly capable of carrying messages and keeping his eyes open; Corporal Pritchard would be able to dress his hand when we got back to the houses. One of Gray's men, his cheek laid open by a mortar splinter, had followed Harrison's example.

Their offer was not refused. Both men required medical attention, but everyone was needed out there on the perimeter. In any case, I could not do without Harrison. Put simply, I just needed the man there to look after me, to bolster my own failing reserves of strength. Harrison was as indispensable as it was possible for anyone to be.

My request to withdraw Gray's platoon seemed to surprise the General. He did not admit it, but it sounded as if he had not realized that men were still fighting out there on the edge of the park; there was no doubt at all that he knew that the units on either side of us had gone. Perhaps everyone had just assumed that the platoon had withdrawn as well – or had been wiped out. Or had it just been forgotten? It was all a little vague, but it was pointless to probe. After all, the General had a lot to think about, and he was the last man to be careless about his troops.

Large, quiet, imperturbable figures were a comfort to have around in battle, and the General, in some ways a little like Harrison, was just such a person. His news, however, was in no way comforting, but he paid me the compliment of not trying to put a gloss on the unpleasant facts. Nothing had been heard from the bridge for the past twenty-four hours; even if some survivors were still holding out there, they could hardly last much longer. The Polish Brigade had been dropped a few hours before on the flat polderland south of the river, and with luck it should be possible to ferry them across on rafts during the night. Otherwise, except for the medium guns, there was no help in sight for the troops crammed into this ever-shrinking perimeter in Oosterbeek. The 2nd Army still seemed to be as far away as ever. The General did not say as much, but his tone of voice showed that he felt the same as the rest of us about those dilatory armoured and infantry divisions.

It was a surprise to discover that Brigade HQ was again functioning, with our Brigadier in charge of all the troops on the east side of the perimeter. It seemed odd that nobody had told me. Last night I had received my orders direct from the General, so this evening I had made my way again to Hartenstein to find out what we should do, nobody having been in contact with us all day. It was the usual muddle of war.

One of the General's staff guided me to Brigade HQ. As far as could be seen in the dark, it consisted of only a few holes in the ground, about a couple of hundred yards from Hartenstein, which provided shelter for two staff officers, half-a-dozen men and the Brigadier himself. It was far from being a salubrious spot. Snipers had been active all day and there was no shelter from either tree bursts or the rain, which was now teeming down. Foul though life might be on the perimeter, in some ways it was preferable to this place.

The Brigadier had been hit in the face during the day by a splinter from a mortar bomb which had killed his new brigade major, a staff officer loaned to him from Division, but he was still able to smile through his bandages and seemed to be as ebullient as ever. He had nothing to add to the General's instructions to me that Jimmy's platoon should be withdrawn and concentrated with the rest of the Battalion in the street behind, but it was nice to see him and to talk to him again. Neither rations nor ammunition were to be had, but the Brigadier was able to produce half-a-dozen stragglers belonging to the Battalion, very welcome reinforcements, particularly Corporal Day, the tough young transport NCO who was in charge of them.

The discovery that there was no food made me aware once more of a stomach which was very empty indeed. As our party edged its way back to the others, first through the Hartenstein grounds, then the dash across the main road,

151

followed by the cautious progress through the silent side streets, it was hard to keep my mind off that last and only meal, eaten over twenty-four hours before. During the day I had been too busy to remember my hunger, but the knowledge that there were no rations had reawakened a dormant appetite in a most perverse manner.

It was nearly half-past nine before we were back at headquarters. After replying to the rather shaky challenge of the nervous sentry dug in at the hedge near the corner of the road, I entered the house. Immediately I sensed that something had changed. The house hummed with talk. Swinging open the kitchen door, I saw three men sitting round the square table, their faces dim in the light of a single candle. John Simmonds and Colour-Sergeant Bower I had expected to see, but the third man was Jimmy Gray.

It was a relief that Jimmy made no attempt to apologize for what had happened. It had been a deliberate decision. Twice enemy patrols had approached the corner house and twice they had been driven off. When still no word had come, two hours after the party of wounded had left, Jimmy had decided that something was wrong and that he had better pull his men back to join the others, conscious as he was that in daylight they would stand little chance out there by themselves with the enemy all around them.

Jimmy had been wrong, but I could not bring myself to blame him for what he had done. There was no excuse for withdrawing without permission, but such an order could have gone astray. Or my party of wounded and myself could have been wiped out on the way back. It stood to reason that someone, sometime, should pull them back from that isolated corner, although in battle reason is not always the overriding consideration. But as it turned out, Jimmy had managed to bring all his men back safely without the enemy discovering they were leaving.

Already Jimmy had settled his men into the three houses on the right of the other platoon, an arrangement which there was no reason to change. The Battalion now held a solid block of small detached dwellings which lined either side of the single short street. Beyond the road junction on our left was the Recce Squadron, but on the other flank, there was no one at all, just empty houses. Only then did it strike me that there was nothing behind us either. To the north of Div HQ, between the staff and the Boche, there was only this single street of defended houses. A perimeter they called it, and a perimeter it was, a single line of fighting men with nothing in the rear except a few guns, together with bits and pieces of headquarters staff and RASC. It seemed to be one colossal bluff.

Food was now the dominant problem. Listening to the sound of smashing glass, clear above the noise of the rain, as Jimmy Gray prepared his houses for defence, I talked to Bower about it. While I was away, he had recieved one small windfall. A Dutch shopkeeper had emerged from his cellar to show him a British jeep, parked in a garage in the next street with its load intact. By an odd coincidence, it belonged to our own machine-gun officer, but there was no way of telling how it had got there or what had happened to the driver. Most of the contents were of no use, machine-gun instruments and spares, but there were 4,000 rounds of ammunition and a couple of cases of Compo rations, a day's food for sixteen men, as well as the officer's small pack with his forty-eight hour ration pack intact inside it. Altogether it was a useful find.

But this was not much among fifty men. The only thing to do was to forage among the houses, although the chances of finding much were slim indeed after four years of war and rationing.

The foraging party, with Bower in charge of it but Private

Jones very much the inspiration, was back within the hour bearing a variegated collection of provisions, but enough when added to the Compo to make a reasonable meal for everyone. Few houses had been found to be empty. Each one had a cellar, and nearly every cellar sheltered a Dutch family. The empty houses were bare of provisions except for a few bottles of preserved fruit and vegetables, but the Dutch in the cellars, short of food though they were, had nearly all contributed something, a loaf of bread here, a piece of cheese or a few potatoes there.

We should, of course, have been more ruthless and impounded at least enough to last us through the following day. Food we must have, if we were to continue to fight, but even Jones, with his lack of respect for other people's property, particularly if it belonged to foreigners, had hated asking these open-handed people to give them the food they needed to keep their own children alive. How nice the British could be! Any other race would have taken what they needed with little or no compunction. But there it was!

It was three o'clock before I found the time to sit down in the cellar of the centre house, where Bower, who was now doubling the duties of sergeant-major with quartermaster-sergeant, had placed the headquarters. The savoury mixture of Compo stew, supplemented by fresh potatoes and beans, with a bowl of preserved fruit and a hunk of Dutch bread and cheese to top it all off, lay warmly in my stomach. Drenched clothes were almost forgotten. Perhaps now two or three hours sleep could be snatched before stand-to.

Bower, Harrison and Williams were already unconscious in the corner of the cellar, each wrapped in a Dutch eider-down. Jones, who had cooked the meal, was on sentry-duty, while Galbraith and Jackson were tinkering with the erratic field-telephone which linked us intermittently with the head-quarters in the rear. Two hours before, the Brigadier had

154

been through with final orders for the next day. We were to hold where we were, taking the Recce under command. This had involved another visit to them, the second time that night I had been around the area. They were an impressive bunch of people to have with one, among the best troops in the Division, tough, intelligent and well-disciplined. I was confident that they would stay in those houses whatever happened.

On the way back, as Bower and I approached the sentry-post at the road junction, we had expected to be challenged. Nothing happened. We stopped on the far side of the road, and Bower whispered softly across to the sentry, thinking that the man had not heard us. Still all was quiet. The two of us looked at one another. What had happened? When we had passed the corner thirty minutes earlier, everything had been in order. Was the sentry all right?

Motioning to Bower to cover me, I stood up and tip-toed across the road, Mauser ready, its safety catch pushed forward. In the trench a shape was visible, slumped across the parapet. To one side lay the unattended Bren gun. It was a young soldier of 'A' Company, a man I hardly knew, fast asleep.

However exhausted the poor devil was to have allowed himself to fall asleep, it was a crime impossible to overlook. A salutary lesson was needed to stop the same thing happening again. Shifting the Bren well to one side, I dropped on top of the lad, grasping him around the neck as if to throttle him. With a choked gasp of terror, he squirmed for a moment under me before he recognized my voice. Then I let go, cursing him for his stupidity.

Back in the house, Bower's silent disapproval was only too apparant. Perhaps the lesson had been too brutal, but I was past niceties of behaviour. Perhaps I had been wrong, probably so. But to stay awake in our present state needed a conscious effort of will, and a sleeping sentry endangered us all. The man would not do the same again. In other armies men were shot for such a crime. It was easy enough to be critical when the ultimate responsibility was not your own.

CHAPTER SIX

DEFIANCE

It was Friday. For the first time since we landed we seemed to be in control of the situation, not pieces of drift-wood swept between abyss and whirlpool. Across our side of the perimeter we had built a breakwater, not solid but secure enough.

The day had begun at dawn with a prolonged and intense bombardment from a battery of Nebelwerfers, vicious six-barrelled mortars, even more frightening than the usual ones, possibly because they gave such a prolonged warning of their intentions. The multiple thump of firing was followed by the whine of the six descending bombs, which rose to a scream before they burst in shuddering patterns around the houses. All the hate of the battle seemed to be packed into that scream; each cluster of bombs might have been a senti-ent being engaged on searching for its own living target among the houses and gardens. But the houses sheltered us, and the bombs did little more than eat further into our depleted reserves of courage. All day, only two men were wounded by this bombing, and by the intermittent shelling and mortaring which followed. One or two snipers were busy, but they failed to hit anyone. A more serious threat was an SP gun which twice edged down a side road towards us. It was cautious, however, pulling back each time after blowing a hole or two in the houses, wary of coming within range of the Piats.

The Battalion was holding both sides of the Paul Kruger-straat. Joubert Weg and Botha Weg nearby were further ironic reminders of other men who, at the turn of the century, had fought the British Army. The houses must have been built at about the same time. They were pleasant little places, the homes of clerks and small tradesmen, two or three storeys high, gabled at the top and with cellars beneath. Each had its own back garden with flowers and a vegetable plot; in front a further narrow strip was edged by a waist-high fence, cast-iron and spike-topped, often backed by a thick laurel hedge, testy little obstacles to cross at speed.

Just after the bombardment ended, a party of glider pilots arrived with orders to occupy the houses on our right and to place themselves under my command. Even more welcome reinforcements reached us a little later in the shape of the Quartermaster and twenty men of the Battalion whom the Brigadier had collected from various corners of the Divisional area. Most of them had landed by glider with the transport; some had been dropped astray and had only just turned up; others had become separated from the Battalion during the first few hours of fighting. All of them seemed glad to be back with their own unit, among their friends, with officers whom they knew. By comparison with us, they were quite fresh, having had more time to sleep and to forage for food. Including the Recce Squadron and the glider pilots, I was now in command of about a hundred men, our task to defend a stretch of the perimeter nearly six hundred yards across, the larger part of the northern flank of the area held by the Division. It was a small enough force for the job.

I was a little worried by the glider pilots when I walked across to see them in their houses. They were intelligent young men, individualists, skilled in an esoteric art, but they were pilots first and infantry soldiers afterwards. As I talked to the staff-sergeant in charge, the rest started to gather around in ones and twos, interested in what we had to say, but clearly disagreeing with some of it. They seemed disposed to discuss orders, perhaps because the orders came from a complete stranger, butting in on the conversation with their staff-sergeant. They were finding it a little difficult to accept this major who had appeared out of the blue and was now telling them what to do in a perhaps rather uncompromising manner. This easy-going approach was understandable, but in the circumstances it was hard to sympathize with it. The only way for us all to survive was for everyone to do what they were told and to do it quickly. The trouble was that these pilots were strangers. Their loyalties were to one another, and there was no reason why they should have any confidence either in me or in the men of the Battalion. They accepted the orders, but with an ill grace, and I left them conscious that I could have handled them better. But I was beyond finesse and tact. I was too tired; there was still so much to do.

Again we were all famished. Except for a few boiled sweets and a little bottled fruit, the last tins of food had been eaten early that morning, hardly enough for more than a mouthful each. The lack of tea was an even greater deprivation. Towards the end of the morning I sent the Quartermaster back to Hartenstein with two or three men to see if they could find anything to eat, but they returned empty-handed. No one else, it appeared, had anything to eat either.

Because there was little for him to do in his own trade, I decided to appoint the Quartermaster as adjutant to the force. Hugh Elkins was not the standard quartermaster, the elderly RSM promoted to administrative duties, but a youngish man, little more than thirty, promoted only a short time before from one of the technical corps. Although he had never served with the infantry and had not parachuted before, he had settled down quickly in the Battalion. His pleasure now at finding us again after the four days of separation was uninhibited. Lucky enough still to possess some untouched reserves of energy, Hugh flung himself with zest into his new duties.

Inside the houses we were reasonably safe from shells and bullets, but there was always some cause for the officers and senior NCOs to move about in the open from one building to another. It was the same as it had been in the woods. The officers and sergeants stood a greater chance of being killed or wounded than their men. All the same, it was easier for an officer. With so much to do, he had little time to worry about his own safety. Also, he always had to try to act a part, to set an example to the others. An officer had to exude confidence, however hard it might be, but because he always had to try to keep a grip on himself, it helped him to forget the danger.

So perhaps the cool courage of Corporal Galbraith and Private Jackson, the two signallers, was all the more praiseworthy. The Battalion's sole link with the rear was the single field telephone line. Whenever the line went dead, Galbraith and Jackson had to climb the cellar steps, walk out of the back door, and follow the snaking cable through the gardens and across the roads until they found the break. Time and again that day the line was cut by shell or mortar fire, and backwards and forwards along its length walked the two signallers, carrying their heavy drums of cable, searching for the breaks and mending them. Not once did they have to be told to go, nor did they make more than a perfunctory, blasphemous complaint before doing so. It was their routine job, and Jackson was just nineteen years old. With snipers

160

watching for them, and bombs and shells bursting around them, their continued survival was inexplicable.

A further visit to the Brigadier in the dark of that Friday night produced little in the way of fresh news. There had been rumours during the day that all resistance at the bridge was over. The Brigadier confirmed that this was true. The previous morning the last few survivors clinging to the north end of the bridge had all been overrun. It had also been a bad day for the troops holding the southern end of the perimeter. All through the hours of daylight the Boche had been trying to cut them off from the river, but in this they had failed. Nevertheless the attacks had in part been successful and tonight the perimeter was that much smaller. Neither of us mentioned the possibility of relief. It seemed so unlikely now. In any case, it hardly seemed to matter any more. I felt with a fatalistic feeling that we would just fight on until we were all killed, or until the ammunition ran out. It had happened at the bridge, and now it would happen here.

Standing in the shadow of one of the large Hartenstein trees, I was saying good-night to the Brigadier when one of our armoured carriers clattered past towards the main road. The occupants were invisible in the dark, but the Brigadier was certain that the driver was Paul Lewis, the Battalion's carrier platoon subaltern. For the past two days Paul had been ferrying wounded men in that flimsy carrier, open-roofed, with armour thick enough only to stop a rifle bullet, driving backwards and forwards between Div HQ and the two dressing stations at the crossroads. Sometimes the Boche shot at him deliberately because they did not see the red cross draped across the engine, but the casual mortar and shell fire, and the machine gun bullets channelled along the broad main road never ceased. Although the Germans were trying to respect the red cross flag, it was

161

hard to understand how Paul had managed to survive for so long.

I remembered then that Paul was a Jew, a car dealer from somewhere up Golders Green way, the only one of his race among the officers, a man who did not try to pretend to be something else but was proud of being a Jew. There had been few others in the Battalion, probably not more than half a dozen or so. Ticking them off in my mind, I realized that all of them, with the exception of one who had not arrived, had caught my attention during the battle. The Jews must have even more to fight for than the rest of us. Certainly they had more to revenge.

It was late that night by the time I returned from seeing the Brigadier, and later still by the time I had once again been around the positions. Tonight there were no sleeping sentries.

I should have managed to get some sleep, but in the end I snatched no more than an hour or so. Every time I dropped off, something or other happened to rouse me. Three or four times in the early hours, Boche patrols were caught probing down side roads or across gardens, dim figures in the light of Verey flares as they sought safety from the red tracer bullets of the Brens.

The noise started just before dawn. It was not the first time we had heard it since we arrived in Oosterbeek, but now it went on and on, chilling us with apprehension. It was the clatter of tracks on paved and cobbled roads, insistent even above the roar and throb of the heavy engines. Heavy armoured vehicles, tanks or SP guns, were moving into the outskirts of the town, ready for the next day's fighting, taking advantage of the cover of darkness. We knew what this portended. We could probably withstand a lot more shelling and mortaring, and, from the shelter of these houses, we had the advantage of the enemy infantry.

But against armour we could do little or nothing. I remembered the damage the gun had done to the house down the road, outside which Luke Tyler had died.

At stand-to, half an hour before first light, I climbed up from the cellar to take my place with Harrison next to Lance-Corporal Williams' Bren at the back of the first-floor front bedroom. In the dark chill of the early morning, unrested and empty-bellied, it was hard to avoid shivering. The thought of the day ahead filled me with unease. From behind the earth-filled wardrobe lying lengthways across the room, through the empty window-frame a small dark house on the opposite side of the road was barely visible. It held a section of Gray's platoon. Just to the left some trees began to take shape through the murk of drizzling rain. It was part of an orchard, separated from the narrow road in front by a tall iron fence, too high to climb. Through a gap in this fence, a metalled drive, wide enough to take a horse and cart, cut through the middle of the trees.

At last it was fully light. Stand-to would end in five minutes, and then a little sleep might be snatched. At least, I could stretch myself to bring some warmth back into my frozen limbs. But a succession of distant thuds, followed by that all too familiar whistle, suggested that it was not to be. The Nebelwerfers were starting their morning hate.

The first salvo exploded down the road, near the glider pilots, but the next was closer, straddling Simmonds' houses on the left. In a few minutes the salvoes were following each other so closely that the scream of the approach of one group intermingled with the explosions of its forerunner, the various sounds all but indistinguishable. The bombardment was far worse than yesterday's, and it showed no signs of stopping. Other types of mortars and guns joined in,

163

pounding the line of our positions and the empty houses behind. Those Boche patrols last night had pinpointed our front in a very efficient way. The building adjoining the dark house opposite started to burn. Luckily it was unoccupied. Twice bombs hit the roof of our own house, the concussions showering us with plaster, but otherwise harming no one. Further up the street, the side of a roof caved in; a figure appeared for the moment at a window and waved, possibly in reassurance.

This was more than a routine early morning stonk. The Germans must be softening us up in preparation for something more serious. Their ammunition seemed to be unlimited.

The bombardment ended quite suddenly, rather as it had started. This would be it. Nudging Williams to get his head up from behind the barricade, I shouted a warning to the others – Elkins and Bower in the next room and the two signallers who had moved up into the bedroom at the back. The stutter of a Bren cut across the words. Bower's rifle thudded next door, and then Williams was firing a succession of bursts from his Bren gun. In the orchard opposite, Germans were running through the trees towards us. Several dropped. This could only be the start of an attack. Now, from either flank, the sound of rifles and machine-guns reached us, accompanied by the thud of exploding grenades. The attack was coming in all along our front.

Some of the Germans among the fruit trees were firing back; a couple of rifle bullets splintered the front of the wardrobe. Then more grey figures were lumbering towards us through the trees. Some fell, others ducked behind the puny trees. They didn't stand a chance. It was like shooting at targets on the practice range. The German guns and mortars had been forced to stop because their troops were so close, so it was possible to fire slow, carefully aimed shots, with little or no distraction. The only way out of the orchard was through the single gap in the high fence, but the enemy soldiers never got within twenty yards of it.

A tall German officer was standing in the middle of the drive, out in the open clear of the trees, waving his arm to the men behind him. It was like an illustration from the *Boy's Own Paper*. No more than fifty yards away, every detail of his face and uniform was clearly visible. He was a handsome young man, fair-haired and smartly turned out. Already he had been standing there for about five seconds, encouraging his men to advance.

As I levelled my sights on the German officer, I knew that I was looking at someone who was just about to die. It seemed a pity. He was such a courageous boy, just the sort one would have liked as a platoon commander. My finger started to squeeze the trigger, but it was too late. Someone else had fired. The German fell, spreadeagled, and lay still. At least he had died quickly.

The death of the young officer marked the end of the attack. No one now moved in the orchard except for a single wounded man squirming his way back through the trees. In a minute or two the firing on either flank died away as well, only the odd rifle shot or burst of machine-gun fire breaking the silence.

As we crouched behind our weapons, waiting for the next German attack, two figures, just visible at the back of the orchard, started walking down the drive towards us. There was no need to hurry; there would be plenty of time to kill them when they were fully in view. Then I noticed that they were carrying something between them – a stretcher. Harrison's gasp of admiration filled the room. They were not even waving a white flag, just walking calmly into our field of fire to pick up their wounded. Then something else struck me: the Germans would hardly behave like that unless they were confident that they would not be shot at. It would be different on the Russian front. I prayed that none of our men would open fire, either purposely or in error.

Deliberately the two Germans lowered their stretcher to the ground by the side of a crumpled figure, slid it on to the canvas, and then raised their burden. By then, two more pairs of stretcher-bearers were coming down the drive. In the space of about fifteen minutes, a dozen wounded men were removed from the orchard. Not a shot was fired. I wondered how many dead lay there among the trees.

After the German wounded had been taken away, little happened for the next couple of hours. The lull gave me a chance to visit everyone. Two men had been killed and another three wounded in Simmonds' platoon, all of them crushed by the side of a house which had collapsed under a direct hit from a shell. Gray's platoon had escaped un-scathed, despite the fact that the men of one section had used hand grenades to beat back some Germans who had managed to reach the back door of their house. Two of the Recce had been wounded, but no glider pilot had been hit. The success had done a lot of good. Everyone seemed confident – cocky, in fact – particularly the glider pilots, about whom there was no longer any need to worry.

But as I walked from one house to another, dodging from wall to wall, or creeping with Harrison under the cover of the garden hedges, I kept on thinking about the German armour, the sound of which had disturbed us in the dark hours. The outcome of that last attack would have been so very different if the Boche had used the tanks and SP guns to support the infantry. Why had they not done so?

My injured hand no longer hurt; I had not even noticed it when I had been firing the Mauser, unlike yesterday when it had been hard to hold the rifle steady. Under that black and filthy dressing, the wound must be nearly healed. How long ago had Corporal Pritchard bandaged it? Five days now! The colour of the dressing matched the protruding ends of the unwashed fingers, and the skin of the other hand was the same, a dull, greasy grey, the dirt ingrained and shiny. Rubbing a hand across my bearded chin, I wondered what I looked like. Shaving every day! Involuntarily I laughed at the conceit, surprising Harrison who gave me a rather odd glance. Even if there had been time for such frills, we needed the water for drinking; the taps were all dry, the water cut off at the mains, probably deliberately so by the Germans. All of those around me, including the boys of nineteen, looked middle-aged, the etched lines of weariness in their faces highlighted by the infilled filth. Perhaps that was why that clean and well-shaven German officer looked so very young, standing there alone in the middle of the orchard.

The mortaring started again as we regained the comparative security of the headquarters house. A flurry of shots and bursting grenades from the direction of Gray's flank propelled me up the stairs to see what was happening. Crouched next to Lance-Corporal Williams, at first I could discern nothing, but by venturing forward to the corner of the window, trusting that no sniper was watching, it was just possible to catch a glimpse of the cross-roads where Gray's position met that of the glider pilots. There was nothing visible except a couple of dead Germans lying in the middle of the road, but now there was another noise, penetrating through the din of the mortars and machine-guns. It was the menacing clatter of tracks on the hard roadway, only the single vehicle apparently, but a very large one from the deep roar of its engine.

The cough of the gun was one with the noise of the explosion which reduced the corner of the house at the cross-roads to rubble. As the gun fired for the second time, blowing off the side of the roof, two men in red berets darted out of the front door and across the road. Lacking the means to retaliate, they could not be blamed for leaving. Then it appeared. Around the side of the shattered house poked the muzzle of a vast gun. It fired once again, this time towards the house on the other corner occupied by the glider pilots. It was possible now to see enough of the tank to be able to recognize it, not that I had ever confronted one of the type before. Of all things, the Boche had brought their Tigers, the largest of all their tanks, into the streets. Again the gun fired, and again there was a crash of falling masonry.

Without warning, the side of the tank's turret was splashed with flame. Again the massive engine roared into life as the hulking monster reversed into the shelter of the house. Gray's men must have hit it with their Piat, the only one they had. The tank might not have been badly damaged, but the explosion must at least have terrified the crew.

One after another, two phosphorus bombs burst in the road, spreading their pall of dense white smoke towards the houses. Under cover of this clinging screen, two men darted back across towards the enemy and dived for shelter into the door of the shattered house behind which the tank was sheltering. A couple of minutes later a face appeared at the gap in the roof. It was Private Robertson, his rifle slung over his shoulder, a large object in his hand. The head vanished. Still there was no noise from the tank. Behind, two of Simmonds' Brens were firing.

Then a deep explosion resounded from the place where the tank was hidden. Five seconds later there was a second. Something spiralled into the road to explode into another cloud of white smoke, and the two figures were sprinting back through it into the shelter of the house from which they had come. I knew then what they had done. They had leaned out of an upstairs window and lobbed a couple of

168

Gammon bombs, bags of plastic explosive armed with impact detonators, down on to the top of the tank.

In a few minutes, the surmise was confirmed. Private Jones, no longer his ebullient self, but shattered by fatigue, brought a message from Jimmy Gray. The two men had scored direct hits with their bombs. Afterwards the tank had not moved, nor had anyone left it. The crew must be dead or concussed inside their steel shell.

This was a success indeed, a Tiger tank knocked out by a couple of plastic bombs! No one had ever thought that the things would prove lethal to anything more than an armoured car.

But we had won no more than a temporary respite. Fifteen minutes later we could hear the unnerving noise once again. Tracks were clattering towards us. A gun thudded, and the dark red house opposite began to fall apart as round after round crashed into it. Muzzle flashes from the far side of the orchard revealed the position of the attacker, but there was nothing we could do. At least the men were not waiting in the house to be killed, but slipping one after another out of the door, back across the road to the headquarter house. On either side other guns were firing.

Now it was our turn. The first round sent tiles and roof beams crashing into the road outside. The second exploded in the empty room below, throwing us all to the floor. The plaster dust and debris had choked Williams' Bren, but Harrison and the CQMS were still firing round after round from their weapons in a hopeless but determined manner towards the armoured shape in the orchard. It was time to leave. We would all be dead if we stayed any longer. Bawling to the men in the other rooms to get out, I herded everyone down the stairs and out into the back garden, just as the front of the house disintegrated into the road.

Chaotic though it appeared, a semblance of order remained. Everyone seemed to have cleared out of the wrecks of the houses, but I sent the Quartermaster and Bower, one to the left and one to the right to make certain that all were empty. Some men were crouched in the gardens, weapons levelled at the backs of the houses, waiting for the Boche infantry to emerge; others were digging, using entrenching tools, garden spades, pieces of board or even their bare hands. It was not only a relief, but rather astonishing as well, to discover that no one had run further than the back gardens; they could well have broken in panic to disappear among the houses behind.

On the left a Bren fired at a group of Germans exposed for the moment in a gap between two houses. Otherwise nothing happened. The enemy guns were silent. There was neither sight nor sound of the tanks. Perhaps the German armour was wary of venturing further forward among the houses, but it seemed strange that we should be left in peace in this way to scratch our burrows in the garden soil. The enemy had not managed things at all well. First they had allowed their infantry to be slaughtered in an unsupported attack, although their armour was close by. Then the armour had attacked alone without the infantry necessary to winkle us out of the ruins of the houses. War was a succession of disasters, sometimes to one side alone, but more often to both at the same time.

It was time to strike back. The tanks had gone, and as yet the Boche did not appear to have occupied the houses. Lying out there in the rear gardens, overlooked from the windows, we were vulnerable indeed. Soon the mortaring would start again. Then we would be safer back in the ruined buildings.

As John Simmonds listened to the instructions, the young captain's manner was as relaxed as ever. Calm and outwardly self-confident, he somehow managed to give the impression that he was almost enjoying the morning's work. Possibly he was making the point, subconsciously perhaps, that a gunner could always take charge of thirty infantrymen, but there were undoubtedly immense reserves of strength hidden behind that cool exterior. As he lay behind the bed of half-dead pea plants, scanning the houses for any sign of German occupants, there was no trace of disquiet in his voice as he discussed his orders to counter-attack and clear the street of the enemy.

Fifteen minutes after John had gone, I was still in the same place in the vegetable patch, watching the second hand of my watch creep up towards the top of the dial. Then Gray's weapons opened up on the right, firing into the back rooms of the houses, more in the hope of distracting the enemy than providing covering fire. The danger to John's men lay on the other side – the front of the houses. Now John's three Bren guns were firing as well on the left. The assault party would be moving into the street.

It came. The sustained rattle of a Spandau, first one gun, then a second. After that there was silence, except for one or two rifle shots.

I waited, lying in the vegetable patch, almost distraught with worry. Something was badly wrong. Nothing could be seen from here, but I had to resist the temptation of going and finding out for myself what was happening. I must avoid getting involved in the skirmish. Then Corporal Day, now John's second-in-command, was running through the flower-beds towards me. Day's face said everything, even before he started to speak. The attack had failed. It had failed the moment John had been killed, out there in the middle of the street and ten yards in front of Day and the rest of the assault party. John had died in just the same way as that young German officer this morning. That had finished it. The rest of them, including Day, had turned and run, but

171

in some extraordinary way no one else had been hit. Day made no attempt to excuse himself, telling the story factually and not trying to put a gloss upon the incident. The implication was clear: they had been asked to do too much.

So now I had been responsible for killing John as well. It had been so simple. I had issued the orders, and then John had walked out into the middle of that road to be shot down by the machine-gun.

I should not have done it. The counter-attack should never have been attempted. The men were no longer capable of making such an effort. They could still hang on to their positions, fighting from behind cover, but after six days of continuous battle they lacked the will to get to their feet and go for the enemy. In the woods it had just been possible to urge them forward in one last surge of willpower, but since then they had endured a further forty-eight hours of death, starvation, thirst and fatigue. And in the woods it was men from my own company. Today it had been different. Today a mixture of men, survivors of four different companies, had been left to follow a gunner officer whom they hardly knew. There were limits to what soldiers could be asked to do, and I had gone beyond those limits. And so John Simmonds had died.

It was strange that the enemy did not come and finish us off. Our last Piat had been smashed during the tank attack. Now our only defence against the German armour was half-a-dozen Gammon bombs. In the middle of the afternoon, just after John had died, the mortaring had started again and continued ever since. Although for most of the time we had been out in the open, finishing our slit trenches, only two more men had been wounded.

Our headquarters had been sited in a large chicken-run at the end of the garden of the house which we had been holding. At the back of the run was a hen-house, containing

172

half-a-dozen birds, unnoticed by the night-before-last's foraging parties; now there were no fires on which to cook them. It was not too bad a defensive position; the chicken-wire helped to hide the digging, while the field of fire extended right up to the houses, some forty yards away.

The trenches to be occupied by Galbraith and Jackson had been dug for them by the other five members of the headquarters. For the two signallers, today had been a repetition of yesterday. After the second German attack, the telephone line was again found to be dead, cut by the mortar fire, and the two men had been obliged to follow it back until they found the break. Twice more this happened during the early evening. Each time Galbraith and Jackson had dragged themselves from the feeble shelter of the half-dug trenches to search for the gap and mend it, waiting all the time for the sniper's bullet in the back.

Just after the line had been repaired for the third time, the instrument lying in the corner of the newly-dug trench buzzed. It was the Brigadier at the other end, the first time he had managed to contact us all day. From the day-long noise of the battle, and the reports he had received from other units, he realized that we were in serious trouble. Now he wanted to know whether we could hold out much longer. The Brigadier's question sounded as if a negative answer was expected. It was unlike him.

There was little or no point in telling the Brigadier the truth. I knew that we could not stop another tank attack, but decided that I might as well put a bold face on it. What did it matter. The Brigadier would not be able to send help anyway; the situation would be just as bad elsewhere. In any case, I was inhibited in what I could say by the others, sitting only a few feet away, and straining their ears to over-hear the conversation.

So I told the Brigadier that we could hang on, hoping that

the confidence in my voice would not sound too false. I did, however, make the proviso that we must have a couple of Piats and ammunition of every type, and was surprised to receive the reply that the stuff would be produced. Would I come in after dark, bringing a carrying party?

I did not waste the Brigadier's time mentioning the subject of food. It seemed pointless. If he had access to any rations, he would say so. But that afternoon we had again watched the RAF dropping their supplies over the enemy lines, unable either to locate or to hit the perimeter.

Already it was nearly midnight, and we had only just finished distributing the ammunition and the two Piats. It had been another wretched evening, although the rain had at last lifted. During the day the downpour had been no more than a minor inconvenience of life, hardly noticed; now with another night in the open ahead it was quite another matter.

We had started by getting lost. With CQMS Bower and the six men of the carrying party behind me, I had taken the wrong direction in the Hartenstein grounds, and had blundered around for an hour or so from one set of slit trenches to another, cursed by the occupants and in serious danger of being shot by a light-fingered sentry. No one could direct us to Brigade HQ. The last person we had asked for directions turned out to be, of all things, an RAF flight-lieutenant, shot down a couple of days before and deposited inside the perimeter; his prospects might have been better if his parachute had landed him among the enemy, but he seemed to be happy enough, a Sten gun in his hand, helping to man the headquarter defences.

In the end we managed to stumble upon Brigade HQ, now only three or four slit trenches and in a new position altogether, thus explaining why it had been so difficult to find. Nearby was a small hut, and inside it, tidily stacked, were the ammunition and the two Piats, with ten rounds for each of the weapons.

After despatching Bower's party with the stores, I had sat down to talk to the Brigadier, who seemed to be much the same as ever, still quite cheerful, sprightly even. There was little fresh news, but it was a relief to be able to chat to someone once again without the need to weigh every word. Only about a couple of hundred Poles had managed to cross the river and they were to be placed under the Brigadier's orders the next morning; otherwise there was no sign of relief or of help, except that we could now expect to receive more support from the 2nd Army guns.

Walking back across the Hartenstein grounds, I wondered how I had restrained myself from voicing doubts about the planned arrival of the Poles. And even if they did turn up, they would make little or no difference to the outcome. Now we were on our own to fight it out for as long as our ammunition and our spirit lasted. Perhaps the end would come tomorrow, perhaps the day after. It hardly mattered.

Just as we parted, the Brigadier had explained that he had not been to see us because he had been fully occupied with other sectors of his front which were rather less securely held. A few words like that helped a lot!

A troubled Quartermaster met us when we got back to the house. Bower and his party had not arrived. So for forty-five minutes the two of us sat there, powerless to do anything, waiting for the seven men to turn up, expecting the worst. But at last they stumbled in, nearly collapsing under their loads, having lost their way again on the return journey. Nothing, however, had been jettisoned; they had brought back every round of ammunition.

Now perhaps, a little sleep might be possible. Even the

chicken shit at the bottom of that dank wet ditch was enticing. Cold though I was, I could hardly keep awake. Sleep I must have. All evening I had felt light-headed. Soon my judgement would start to fail, if it had not done so already. At least there was a single blanket, looted by Harrison from one of the houses. I started to wrap myself inside it, when the sentry's challenge stopped me. There was a muttered consultation with my own name mentioned.

It was Corporal Day. He had brought the news that John Simmonds was not dead after all, but severely wounded. Some Dutch people were caring for him in one of the houses just behind Day's position.

Day led Corporal Pritchard and me to the house. A frightened middle-aged Dutchman answered our knock. The relief on the man's face was pathetic to see when he recognized us as British; he well knew what the penalty would be for himself and his family if the Germans were to find him harbouring a parachutist.

As the Dutchman led us into the house, we passed the top of the steps leading down to the cellar. At the bottom a flickering candle lit the faces of four children, all huddled together under a quilt, gazing up at the intruders with terrified eyes. The man took us upstairs to the front bedroom.

Propped up in the middle of the bed lay John, fully clothed, his filthy shirt ripped open to show the blood-stained bandages wrapped around his chest. Beside him sat the Dutchman's wife, holding John's right hand between both of hers. John was unconscious, his sweat-covered face the colour of old putty, and he breathed in great rasping gasps. The Dutchman explained that the British officer had been shot more than once through the chest, but it was beyond the scope of his English to explain how John had come to them.

176

For a couple of minutes the three of us stood in silence, listening to John's terrible efforts to draw breath into his shattered lungs. There was nothing which Pritchard could do for him. Nor could anyone else for that matter.

As I turned to go, motioning to the others to follow, I reached for John's free hand to squeeze it.

The sky to the south was red with the glow of burning buildings as I spoke on the telephone to the Brigadier's last surviving staff officer, asking for a jeep to be found to collect John and take him to the dressing station. The voice at the other end promised to do everything possible, but we both knew that it was a charade. Even if there was a jeep, the driver would never find the house in the dark; by day, it would be impossible to drive up that road. We could not get John back ourselves. There were no stretchers left, and even if there had been it was doubtful whether anyone had the strength left to carry John all the way.

It was still dark when a hand shook me awake. It was CQMS Bower to say that John was dead; he had lived only for a couple of hours after we had left him. I was glad that no jeep had come. Better for John to die in that comfortable bed with a woman holding his hand than to be moved once again.

I must have slept for about two hours. Never had I felt so awful, chilled to the bone, clothes still soaked from yesterday's rain. And it was raining once again. Stiff as I was, it was difficult to climb out of the trench, a deep one I was glad to note. I began to scratch, first my chest and then my right leg, but soon I was itching in half a dozen different places. Then it dawned upon me. Fleas! Chickens carried fleas!

The routine early morning stonk started again, exactly on time, today heavier than ever. The lack of any cover overhead made it even more terrifying. The salvoes followed one another at regular intervals, tearing pillars of earth and stones from the gardens. An explosion half-buried Harrison and me in debris, leaving us bewildered and half-concussed. The bomb had burst on the parapet of our trench, no more than a couple of feet from our heads; a few inches to one side and it would have blown us both to pieces. Everyone now, sentries as well, was cowering in the bottom of the trenches, praying for it all to end. It hardly mattered if the enemy did attack. No one would see them coming, but then they were not likely to try to advance through this maelstrom.

It ended as suddenly as it had started. By some extraordinary chance no one had been hurt, despite the intensity of the bombardment. We started to clear the dirt from ourselves and our weapons, blinking our eyes and talking, once again chewing over the only two topics of conversation: the chances of relief and food. It was then that CQMS Bower reached into the capacious pocket of his airborne smock to produce a single ration tin. It held oleomargarine, the foul-tasting grease which few men could bring themselves to eat unless it was disguised with jam. The tin had been left over from the rations issued three days before, and Bower had held on to it in the hope that sooner or later we would find something to spread it on. Now the tin was opened and a spoon was produced, but ravenous though everyone was, only Bower and myself could force ourselves to swallow a little. I managed three spoonfuls before starting to retch, but it made me feel a little stronger.

I was cleaning the spoon in the earth when a small elderly man, dressed in a dark brown suit and a hard business hat, climbed stiffly over the back fence. In one hand he held a bowl of grain. With a rather off-hand nod to us intruders in his chicken-run, he walked across to the hut and placed the feed inside. Then he felt around for any eggs, found none,

178

and departed the way he had come, uncurious and apparently unafraid. He had uttered not a single word.

The mortaring started again when I was on my way back with the Quartermaster from visiting the Recce. Hugh Elkins had been placed in charge of John's platoon the previous evening, and the two of us had been to see how our neighbours were getting along. The Recce, like ourselves, had been driven out of their house by tanks and had taken refuge in the gardens at the rear; like us also, they seemed to be holding fast to their new positions.

It struck me on the way back that if I ever got out alive, I could wiite a useful chapter for a pamphlet on street fighting. The primary lesson would be the importance of holding gardens and not houses when there were any tanks about. I had never heard the point mentioned before.

This fresh mortaring was not too bad. Only the odd rounds were coming over, and there was plenty of time to dive for cover if one of them sounded as if it might drop too close. We dashed across a side street, moving fast to avoid the attention of any Boche sniper who might have it covered.

On the other side, near a house wall, lay three bodies in a circle around the typical shallow depression made by a mortar bomb. All were members of the Quartermaster's platoon, one a driver, one an orderly-room clerk and the third a cook, a man known to me for years. It was incredible that the early morning bombardment should have harmed no one. Then three good soldiers were killed by one stray bomb.

About noon the Germans attacked once again, their assault preceded by another hellish mortar and artillery concentration. We all knew now what such a bombardment signified at this time of the day, and as soon as the guns and mortars lifted, our heads were up ready for the camouflaged figures sliding around the corners of the houses towards our trenches. At first the attack seemed to be directed towards Gray's men at the crossroads, but after a few minutes some Germans were spotted in the upper room of the smashed house at the end of our garden. Then a Spandau started to fire from the back of the room, spraying bullets all around us, but after a long burst from Lance-Corporal Williams's Bren it was silent. Another Boche with a grenade in his hand started down the garden path towards us, but he got no further than five yards from the back door before he fell.

There was a short lull. Then four Germans darted in turn from one side to the other of the ground floor window facing us. Another couple followed. What they were up to, there was no way of telling, but there were a lot of them in the room. Perhaps they were massing there to rush the chicken-run. Or they could be dragging some small gun into the room. Williams fired a full magazine through the window, but nothing moved. If the Boche were crouching against the outside wall, the bullets would do them little harm. Something must be done. The enemy must not be allowed to collect in that house, so very close to us. There was one possibility. One of the two Piats was with Jimmy Gray, but the second was in reserve, ready to be moved to wherever danger threatened. This would be a novel use for a Piat.

Bower had been a qualified instructor in small arms before being promoted to colour-sergeant. A professional, he took his time, dwelling carefully on the aim and squeezing the trigger slowly and firmly. The bomb flew true, straight through the window, to explode on the wall behind. The sheet of flame and smoke gushing back into the garden coincided with the single protracted scream which eddied from the depths of the room. Then there was silence.

After this the Germans avoided the houses, but otherwise

there was little respite. All day long the sniping and mortaring continued, as small parties of Boche worked around our flanks and in among us. By dusk there were only thirty-seven men still fighting. Jimmy Gray and Hugh Elkins were alive, as were Sergeant Weiner and Corporal Day, but they were the only NCOs left in the two platoons. It was impossible to understand why the Germans were not using their armour to support this infiltration by their infantry; if they had done so, all resistance would have collapsed long ago and the tanks would have been on the Hartenstein lawns.

The crushing news that the Brigadier had been badly wounded came through on the telephone just before the line went dead once again. The Boche were now among the houses and gardens which the glider pilots had been holding, and Gray had reported that he was being shot at from two sides at the same time. The Quartermaster also had sent word that the enemy were behind him, and that he had long ago lost all contact with the Recce on his left.

To disengage had been difficult, but we had managed it, although it cost us several more men. Now the survivors had collected into a sort of box position, actually three parts of the circumference of a circle, with the headquarters, still in the chicken-run, at the top of the arc, nearest to the enemy, who seemed to be very nearly all round us.

We were in a private world of our own, alone with the Boche. If it had not been for the rumble of the battle ebbing and flowing behind, the rest of the Division might no longer have existed. The last time I had struggled around the position, crawling and slithering from slit trench to rubble heap, the sight of the men had shocked me. Days ago I had thought that they must be near the end of their tether; yesterday it seemed all but over; but still we had managed to fight for yet another day without a scrap of food to keep us going. And ahead was the prospect of a further wet and freezing night in the open. At least we were not burdened with any seriously wounded men; those who had been hit were either dead or had managed to drag themselves away in the direction of Hartenstein.

A calculated risk had to be taken. If we were to have any hope of fighting on tomorrow, we must get some rest and overhaul our weapons. We would shelter for the night in the houses. As yet the Boche had shown little enthusiasm for harassing us in the dark; last night, in fact, we had been left completely alone. Perhaps the same might happen again tonight, thus allowing us the chance of a few hours' warm sleep before we reoccupied the trenches in the gardens just before dawn. After all, with the Germans moving freely on both flanks, we were no longer part of any perimeter; if such a thing did still exist, it must be behind us now. We were just an isolated pocket of resistance out here alone among the enemy.

I chose three adjacent houses in the street leading back from the crossroads where the Tiger tank had been destroyed. Twenty minutes later everyone was inside, with sentries posted at the back and front doors of each house.

Crowded into the tiny front parlour together with Weiner and four or five of his men were the members of the headquarters staff. Someone produced and lit a candle, sticking it by its grease in the centre of the dining-table which all but filled the room. For the first time for days men slipped their webbing equipment off their shoulders and loosened the camouflaged scarves wrapped around their necks. Cigarettes – our sole remaining comfort – were passed around, and water-bottles were drained in the knowledge that they could be filled again from the full bath which had been found upstairs. Then we started to sort out the contents of our pouches and pockets, piling the bits and pieces on the table: odd rounds of ammunition, grenades, half-empty magazines, pull-throughs, and all the other pieces of minor impedimenta which soldiers need to carry around. Men leaned against the wall, or crouched over the table, their weapons in pieces, cleaning and oiling them by the light of the single candle.

In a vivid red flash, the table exploded in our faces. I dived for the wall, cannoning off someone else, and flattened my body against the skirting board. So this was it. Rigid, waiting for the rending metal splinters, I knew that it was over at last, and I was to blame. A Boche patrol had thrown a grenade through the window.

But there had been no explosion, no more than a hiss. Nothing had followed that blinding flash. The room was pitch black. I was lying there in the dark, unhurt.

Slowly we got to our feet, wary, flinching from the expected blow, voices tight with apprehension. A torch beam hit the table. In the middle, where the candle had been standing, was a large burn mark. Weiner guffawed, too loudly, just as I realized what had happened. The candle had fallen on top of a Gammon bomb, which had been lying on the table, setting fire to the plastic explosive.

If the explosive had been detonated, the room and every-one inside it would have been blown to pieces, but it merely set the bomb alight. And I had seen the bomb there, but had done nothing about it. It was then that I understood the extent of my exhaustion.

A quiet and chastened party finished cleaning their weapons and sorting out the ammunition. Then, with equip-ment adjusted once again and belts fastened, there were still seven hours ahead of us before we need leave the houses for the trenches outside. With the night divided into three watches between myself, Corporal Galbraith and Sergeant

Weiner, I had four full hours for sleep before I took my turn on duty. In the room next door was a feather bed covered with a large soft quilt. No one would grudge my having it.

Someone must have been wrenching at my arm for a full half minute. I knew it, but still could not move, could not drag myself back to total sensibility. Surely I had not been asleep for four hours. Sergeant Weiner's voice seemed to be coming from a long way off. At last I managed to make the effort of will to force my eyes half open. Over by the door, just distinguishable in the candle-light, stood a Lieutenant-Colonel, a vaguely familiar figure. Then it came back to me. It was the Brigadier's successor, someone from Division Headquarters. His name had come through in the message that the Brigadier had been wounded, but at the time there were other things on my mind.

It seemed a miracle that the Colonel had managed to ferret us out without stumbling on a house full of Germans. No one could have told him how to find us, because no one had visited us since we arrived on the perimeter. My heart warmed to the man. Here was someone who was ready to discover for himself what was happening, and to run a considerable risk in so doing. When he started to speak, his manner was right too – tentative and sympathetic, in no way assertive. He even looked good, clean and well-shaven. There must be time for such refinements at Division.

He brought good news too, the startling information that the 2nd Army had at last reached the river. This same night, a battalion of the Dorsets was to be ferried across to re-inforce us. Had we succeeded after all, then? But after the many disappointments of the week, it was important not to hope for too much.

A little later, relaxed once again into the softness of the

184

feather bed, it struck me that this colonel was a perceptive person, one who knew that men must have rest and who appreciated the calculated risk we had taken in sheltering in these houses for the night, a decision which might have proved disastrous for him, trying to find us in the dark. The Colonel could well have complained, but he had not done so.

The flea bites were starting to itch again in the warmth of the bed, but a little thing like that was not going to stave off sleep.

Everything became routine in time, even the early morning mortaring, today rather less intense than usual. Although every explosion made its successor just that little harder to bear, there were no trees overhead to cause airbursts; we were reasonably safe in the trenches except from a direct hit. Also, we were warmer now; my own clothes were at last dry, and under my smock I was wearing a battered old civilian jacket, purloined from the Dutchman's bedroom.

Just after dawn, over the newly mended telephone line, came the summons to attend an 'O' Group at Division at 0800 hours. As I trudged back I wondered why I had not protested at going. Perhaps I was just too tired to argue; but they should have sent the orders forward to me and not deprived my soldiers of their commander at what had proved to be the most dangerous time of the day. Anyway, some sniper would most likely get me on the way back, crossing the main road, a rubble-strewn death-trap of smashed vehicles, hanging telephone lines, broken buildings and corpses, along which the bullets swept all day long.

By day, the Hartenstein park was sordid indeed. Burnt-out trucks and shattered equipment were scattered everywhere among a litter of severed branches and ploughed turf. Heaps of earth marked the parapets of trenches; other mounds, topped with rough wooden crosses, showed where many of the defenders now lay.

As the two of us walked towards the hotel across the broad lawns, some soldiers in a slit trench shouted a warning to take care. The entrance to the building was covered by a snipeı, hidden among the great cedars and beeches, who only a few minutes before had killed someone else approaching the house.

Sniper or no, I still had to get inside, but Harrison could be spared the risk. The terrace would provide shelter to within thirty yards of the house, but after that one would need to trust to speed to cross the short stretch of lawn. Harrison was clearly reluctant to leave me to go on alone, but he did not argue.

Then I was edging forward across the lawn. On the right, outside the front door, three bodies sprawled untidily around a smashed jeep. The men must have only just been killed; otherwise by now their bodies would have been moved. Then I was running, much faster than I would have thought possible, considering the weight of my equipment. The low open window was no obstacle; I took it like a hurdler, although it was not a sport at which I had ever shown any proficiency. I was into the room and safe. The sniper must have been busy elsewhere.

The Colonel who had visited us was working in an office in one of the smaller ground floor rooms. Only the chandeliers remained as a reminder of past elegance. Piles of equipment and stores littered the floor, and a bed had been dragged into one corner.

After a few generalities, the Colonel apologized that the 'O' Group would be delayed a little. The staff were still settling the details of what was to be a rather complicated plan, and it would be a little time before the full orders were ready. The Colonel seemed to be trying to break something gently. And then it came out. It was hard to believe, harder still to understand.

The Division was to be withdrawn over the Rhine that night. It was all over. It had only been possible to ferry about 250 men of the Dorsets over the river before dawn, a profitless addition to the perimeter garrison. The 2nd Army had over-reached itself in trying to get to us, and although the troops were pouring northwards, they lacked the strength to cross the river and continue the advance into Germany. Already the Boche were hammering from the flanks at their narrow lines of communication.

So the operation had failed! Everything had been in vain! It was all waste!

Listening to the outline of what had to be done that night, it was hard to concentrate on the details. The first emotion was grief. And then utter disappointment. The Battalion had been destroyed to no purpose. But the sorrow swelled to rage as I cursed the 2nd Army for their failure. But after a few minutes, relief supplanted anger. Now there was at least a chance that we might escape, although the prospects of surviving the rest of the day and then withdrawing across the river in our present state seemed slim.

The Colonel disappeared, and I settled down to wait for the details of the withdrawal plan. The delay was exasperating. After fifteen minutes, the bed in the corner looked even more enticing; another short nap could only do me good.

Two hours later I awoke to the fragrance of hot food. For some minutes I lay there, savouring the smell and wondering if some would be offered to me, any compunctions about eating other men's rations overcome by the realization that here in Division they still had food while the men on the perimeter had been starving for the past five days. Then a corporal approached the bed, carrying a plate half covered in delicious tinned stew. Suddenly I was very grateful; these men had little enough for themselves, but they were ready to share it with a stranger.

As the final mouthful of stew slipped down, the rumble of gunfire over towards the north of the park swelled into the room. The sound was self-explanatory. While I lay here, eating stew and drinking tea on a comfortable bed, the Battalion was in trouble. I had waited quite long enough for those orders. Any details which had not yet been confirmed would have to be sent forward to us by some means or other.

With a word of apology to the Colonel, who had just returned to the room, I picked up my rifle and stepped out of the window, back towards Harrison.

CHAPTER SEVEN

RETURN

WHEN I told them the news their response mirrored my own reactions three hours earlier. As the words sank in, I could see the disappointment in their weary, blood-shot eyes. They had seen their mates killed or maimed, the Battalion had been wiped out, and even now their chances of escaping alive were remote. Yet they were not to be given the consolation of seeing the tanks and infantry of the 2nd Army driving northwards through the shattered streets. There was no question now of the war being over by Christmas. It had all been a pointless waste.

The muttered chorus of protest rose to a spontaneous, angry babble, full of bitterness about the troops in the south who had failed to relieve us. Above the rest, I heard Sergeant Weiner insisting that we were far from finished and could still hold the bastards off for days.

Then they fell silent, and I sensed the conflict in their minds, as relief supplanted anger, and doubt followed relief – doubt whether such a withdrawal stood any hope of success. It would be so easy for the Germans to cut us down once we were out in the open, away from the security of the walls and ditches.

As I had feared, they had attacked again while I was away at Division, pushing the men out of their weapon pits, back to the row of large houses overlooking the main road. Five more had been lost in the confusion of the withdrawal and now our ammunition was all but finished. But they still had a strange, stubborn confidence, a quite unwarranted belief that they could hold the Boche from these new positions. I did not share it. They had collapsed earlier that morning, and could easily do so again. Behind us there was nothing but the defences of Div HQ.

They were so tired that they had not started to dig fresh positions, nor could I bring myself to force them to do so, despite the danger of having to face another tank attack. It was now forty-eight hours since we had seen any German armour and soon we would be leaving. In the meantime we were safer in these solid houses than out there in the gardens, digging new trenches.

Until this morning we had managed to hold on despite our exhaustion, but now there was a new factor to consider. Since the second day of the battle we had all been resigned to the inevitability of death; mathematically the chances of being wounded or captured were probably higher, but this had hardly entered our heads. Now, with a way of escape opened and the chance to live restored, hope was likely to crack their will to fight on. Their resolution would break. Then, if things again started to go wrong, they would begin to trickle back to the nebulous safety of the river, past the broken suburban villas, the pitted roads, the burnt-out shells of vehicles and the houses full of wounded.

I had to do something. First food – I had been given half a sandbag full of tins before I left Hartenstein. Harrison had already opened them and the contents were now steaming in a kitchen pan over a fire of broken floorboards. It amounted to no more than three or four spoonfuls each, but it was the first food they had eaten for three days and its effect on them bore no relation to the quantity.

190

When the sentries had been relieved and given their share from the pot, I went back up to the first floor bedroom where six or seven men lay slumped against the walls. Standing well back from the large window, I looked for a minute or two across the gardens where we had spent the past two days. There was no sign of any movement. Had the Germans perhaps pulled back?

I asked the men if anyone still had a razor. There was quite an interval before Lance-Corporal Williams' voice broke the silence. He rummaged among his belongings and produced not only a razor, but soap and brush as well, pointing out as he did so that he had not lost his small pack like the rest of the careless bastards around the place. It was the first attempt at humour which anyone had made that day.

Taking off helmet and equipment I pulled the smock over my head, the first time I had removed it during the past week except the moment last night when I put on the Dutchman's jacket. Standing in my shirt-sleeves before the dressing-table mirror, I was horrified by the apparition which confronted me. The last time I had looked in a mirror had been the night I went to bed in the billet in Leicestershire. I was twenty-nine years old then. In front of me now I saw the face of a man of forty-five, lined, bloodshot, grey and haggard.

Although it was a new blade, it was still agony tearing off the thick, dirty stubble in the drop of cold water which Harrison had found, and my skin was sore by the time I had finished. I combed my hair, knotted my tie again, shook some of the dust from my smock before putting it on, and re-adjusted my webbing equipment.

At first no one said anything. They just watched me, some disinterested, some astonished, Sergeant Weiner with cynical amusement. Then Lance-Corporal Williams took back the shaving tackle and started on his own face. Then the Colour-Sergeant produced another razor from his pocket. Williams

191

even had some spare blades, and soon the two razors were being passed from hand to hand, the men swearing in exasperation as they sawed at their faces and stemmed the blood flowing from the cuts. In a couple of hours every man in the party had shaved; no one had needed an order to persuade him to do so.

It made me think of the Colonel lying dead out there in the wood. He had always insisted that everyone must shave every day, regardless of the circumstances. Sometimes the order had seemed rigid, even futile. Until today there had been no time for such niceties, but again one of the lessons which the Colonel had drummed into us had proved to be sound. Much of the lethargy had been dissipated.

Someone had tucked a much-read newspaper in among the rations. I opened it to see the headlines 'SKY MEN WILL KEEP GOING'. Below, in smaller type, were the words 'PATH OF HELL AT ARNHEM'. It was Monday now. The *Daily Express* was dated Saturday. It must have been dropped by air, or brought over by some liaison officer.

The entire front page of the paper was filled with news of the battle, mostly about the airborne divisions, both our own and the American. It was eerie to read about one's own exploits in this way, particularly with the battle not yet over. For the first time we realized how much the battle had caught the public imagination. This sort of stuff seemed to put it in the category of Zeebrugge or Alamein; but perhaps Dunkirk or Mons might be a better simile. I chucked the paper over to Weiner. As I expected, his reactions were vituperative, but there was gratification in the blasphemy. The paper was a further morale-booster.

The afternoon faltered on towards its uncertain dusk. Of the men not on duty some slept as if drugged; the tension kept others awake, talking, tinkering with their weapons and kit, or pottering aimlessly about the half-smashed

192

house, examining the possessions of its absent owners.

The business of wrapping their boots in strips of blanket cut from the tidy Dutch beds helped to pass the time and provided a topic for banter. By now the laughter was sounding easy – not in any way forced. It was a little like that first night, the sensation of being on yet another training exercise – now nearly over which they were preparing to end with one last effort of disciplined will-power before they returned to the comfort of hot food and warm blankets in their billets. Training had conditioned them to accept discomfort, thirst, hunger and fatigue as a part of life, some sort of preparation for what they had undergone during the past week. Fear and sorrow had been the new ingredients, although there had been little time to spare for sorrow. Now there was a chance of escape. It was strange how natural the laughter sounded.

As the evening shadows lengthened, a few perfunctory rounds of mortar fire crashed harmlessly around the houses, but otherwise the afternoon had been quiet. There was still no sign of life. Perhaps the Germans too had fought themselves to a standstill. Or had they already learned that a withdrawal was being planned? Were they preparing to smash us as we left the security of our positions?

I went over in my mind the details of the instructions as I waited for the officers and NCOs to collect in the sitting room. Williams was already there with Colour-Sergeant Bower, the latter as brisk and business-like as ever. Hugh came next, confident now in his unaccustomed role of platoon commander. Then Jimmy Gray, struggling to shrug off a little of his weariness, with Weiner, Galbraith, Day and Pritchard. Their faces had once again been dirtied, this time with soot to hide them in the darkness. I motioned to them to make a circle on the floor around me.

Further details of the plan for the withdrawal had arrived

over the telephone. In my mind I pictured how it should all happen. Just after dark the sections occupying the two out-lying houses were to collect in the central one where we now were. The Colour-Sergeant would reconnoitre the way back to Hartenstein, to a point where a glider-pilot guide would meet us and lead us down to the Rhine, following tracks marked with white parachute cord. Assault boats manned by Canadian sappers would be waiting there to ferry us across to the other side. It all sounded very simple. If we could creep away without the Boche discovering what was happening, we had little to fear. But there were now some two thousand or so men packed into a strip of land no more than six to eight hundred yards wide and a thousand deep. Some of these men had lost their leaders, and with them their discipline, so silence would not be easy to enforce.

It was all but dark. Standing in the hall of the house, there was a new sound, the shriek of a host of shells passing overhead before they crashed around the houses where we had been fighting for the past five days. It was a moment before I realized that the 2nd Army guns were laying a barrage, trying to mislead the enemy into thinking that the fire heralded a fresh British assault across the river.

As Jimmy Gray's party left the house next door, a building on the left, about a hundred yards away, burst into flames, lighting the garden like day. Caught in the open in the middle of the garden, they all dived for the cover of some laurel bushes, but nothing happened. Through the gap where the hall window had been, I could see them lying there, and I couldn't help thinking of the Germans cringing in their slit trenches, waiting for our artillery to lift. Then Jimmy moved, the others following. In half a minute they were all safe inside the house.

194

By a quarter past eight we were ready to start; being the furthest troops from the river we were the first to leave our positions. With Jimmy and the Colour-Sergeant in front, we stepped out of the back door into the garden, padding in silence, our boots muffled in the blankets and our loose equipment tied into place to prevent rattles. In his left hand each man gripped the unfastened tail of the airborne smock of the man ahead, and in his right he held his weapon. Caught in the glare from the flaming house, we looked like grotesque children playing some macabre party game. I decided to bring up the rear. From the back of the column, I would know if anyone was hit or dropped out.

First we had to cross the main road. As instructed, the men had gathered by the gap in the fence, ready to rush across in a tight mob with Gray and the Colour-Sergeant leading. To try to reach the other side in ones and twos would be impossible; the first men to cross would alert the Spandau crews which covered its length.

At Gray's hissed command we burst across the road in a compact bunch and threw ourselves in a heap on the other side behind the shelter of some trees. As the last few men dropped, two Spandaus found the range; a second too late the stream of scarlet tracer all but brushed our heels before floating lazily away into the darkness of the woods beyond Hartenstein.

Now Jimmy was leading our incongruous crocodile diagonally through the woods which bordered the Hartenstein park. Here the light from the burning buildings and the flares penetrated only with difficulty. The thin rain which had been falling when we started had grown into a harsh, wind-swept downpour, and the stars were hidden by a canopy of black rushing clouds.

A sentry's hoarse challenge sprang out of the bottom of a bush, demanding that one of the men ahead should advance and be recognized. Jimmy moved forward to exchange the passwords, first 'John' and then 'Bull', the responses sounding stilted and theatrical among the wet trees. Again I was reminded of small boys playing soldiers!

The guide was waiting for us a few yards behind the sentry, a tall, thin glider-pilot sergeant, his voice a little tense, worrying perhaps that he might miss the way.

Now we were in the middle of the park and the burning buildings in the distance lit the sky with a dim reflected light. On our right was a high wire-mesh fence. It was the tennis-courts. Among the shapes of the prisoners on the other side, I suddenly distinguished the details of a face, pressed up against the wire, alert with a mixture of anticipation and fear. The Germans had seen what was happening, and the man knew that he could soon be free if he managed to survive the night.

Then the pilot was leading us out of the Hartenstein grounds and into a wood, along a soft track which cut steeply down-hill. Other troops were now moving both ahead and behind, uncannily silent as their muffled feet sank into the soil. There was no sign at all of poor discipline or panic. The plan seemed to be working well.

The line of men was now jerking in a staccato and tiring manner. Every pause by the leaders because of some hold-up in front brought the column to a juddering halt. Then, when it started again, those in front seemed to move too fast so that the ones at the back were all but running to keep up.

Eventually we emerged from the woods, moving down a steep, narrow road, bordered by small suburban houses. I reckoned that we must now be nearing the flat polderland which edged the river. From away in the distance two Bofors guns were pumping red shells towards us at regular intervals, marking the direction for us and decorating the sky in an oddly gay fashion.

196

The men in front suddenly swung wide as if to avoid something. As I came level with the place, I saw the body of a woman lying across the footpath outside the open gateway of a small villa. She lay face uppermost, showing no sign of any injury. She was slim and handsome. Her attitude was strangely graceful, reminding me of some romantic painting of a scene of battle or massacre, absurdly clean and tidy, fit to decorate a decent Victorian parlour. She was so neat, her skirts arranged decorously about her legs, her face calm and unmarked, so different from the torn and bloodied corpses to which we had grown accustomed during the past week. She could not have been there long, and the jug by her side suggested that she had left her house to find water for her family. Among all the dead of the battle, it was the first civilian I had seen.

As I looked away from the woman, I realized that there was no one behind. Either the unit which had followed us out of Hartenstein had branched off down a different path, or the pace had become too quick so that it had dropped behind. Then the column stopped once again, and Sergeant Weiner was beside me.

Weiner was all but inarticulate with rage. He had dropped back to report that the column had split, the fault of Private Oswold, the storeman, who had let go of the tail of the smock of the man ahead, and then had not said anything. The dozen men in front of Oswold, including both the other officers and the Colour-Sergeant, had all disappeared into the night.

A chatter of nervous German from a mound about thirty yards to our left interrupted Weiner's imprecations against Oswold. A Spandau ripped its stream of metal towards us, and we threw ourselves on our faces, most of the bullets flying harmlessly overhead, except for those which ricochetted from the walls and fences. From a few yards away came a long choking gasp. There was a pause. Then Harrison turned his head to say that Private Jones was dead, shot through the chest – Jones, that stout, dependable rogue, seemingly indestructible.

I saw that there was no parachute cord along the path. That poor fool Oswold had led us off the route. Somehow we had to get out of this trap. Since the first burst of fire which had killed Jones, no one had moved. The Boche were still shooting high, uncertain as to our exact whereabouts, their nervousness clear from the wildness of their fire and the chatter of queries and orders which punctuated it.

Slowly I got to my feet. Then I motioned to Sergeant Weiner to do the same, but to stay at the rear. Moving slowly along the line, past Jones' corpse, I pulled each man in turn to his feet. In a couple of minutes all of them were upright, but crouching as low as they could to avoid the bullets which seemed to be flying only inches over their heads. It was a risk, but I could see no other way of starting them all off together and not leaving half of them lying there in the dark.

It worked. They moved off as one man, and in less than a minute we were round the bend, safe from the bullets still being pumped aimlessly into the sky.

Ahead was a church. I had heard that there had been some heavy fighting there. Then the track through the graveyard faded into a field, but the red shells from the Bofors still pointed the way. Soon we were crossing the polderland and I knew that we were nearing the river. A metalled path glistened in the reflected glare from the burning houses on the hill behind us and I stepped on to it from the grass, wondering why I had not noticed it on the map.

My foot disappeared through the surface of the path and I stumbled forward waist-deep into cold water. It was not a path at all, but a small drainage ditch, full to the brim from the night's rain. Tiredness had so dulled my senses that I could not tell asphalt from water!

Floundering to the other side of the ditch, I grabbed hold of a tree and pulled myself out of the water. Behind me, the rest splashed across, holding their weapons high to keep them dry. We plunged on over the water-logged meadows, stumbling and noiselessly cursing, but keeping together, knowing that survival depended on doing so. Ahead there was a high embankment. Fifty yards away was the river, dark and fast-flowing, its further bank a thin line in the far distance.

I led the way down to the water's edge. Just to the left, pulled up on to a small beach, was a small assault boat with its four man crew lying beside it.

The crew did not move as we approached. Then I saw the gaping hole torn out of the side of the boat, and the ungainly posture of the men. The four sappers were all dead, killed by the shell or bomb which had smashed the boat as they waited for their passengers. There were no other boats. Where were the orderly queues waiting to embark, the boats shuttling backwards and forwards, and all the rest of the paraphernalia of a planned evacuation? Something had gone very wrong.

The rain lashed our faces, splashing in large drops into the river. Every gun in the 2nd Army seemed to be hitting the German positions, and the enemy themselves were retaliating in kind, their shells and mortar bombs sending up spouts of water or, when they exploded in the soggy meadows, blankets of wet mud.

More parties of troops now started to arrive, gathering at the water's edge to survey the dark, empty river. Some lay down hopelessly on the bank; others started to search up and down stream for some means of crossing. A few decided to try to swim. A very large gunner officer, heavily moustached, stripped off his equipment and clothes to stand alone on the bank for some seconds, the rain splashing on his naked body, before he waded into the water and struck out with slow, confident strokes towards the far bank. Against that swift current, it was a long way across; he was already being carried rapidly downstream. I stood watching him vanishing into the darkness, there came a rasp of Spandau fire from the top of the embankment about fifty yards upstream. A man toppled backwards and lay screaming at the edge of the water. Everyone scrambled for the yard-wide beach where a low bank provided some slight shelter from the fire.

Then the firing stopped. Unlike the last party we had encountered, the Boche seemed to be either better disciplined or less frightened, shooting only at targets they could see and not blazing away to keep their coouage up. Had they left or were they waiting for something to fire at? The question was quickly resolved. A babble of talk from under the bank about fifteen yards upstream was answered by a stream of Spandau bullets, some of which splashed into the water only yards from where we lay.

I whispered to Harrison to pass the word along to shut up, and heard the murmur of the message being passed from mouth to mouth along the line of men lying under the bank. The babble continued. Taking a chance, I raised my voice to shout for silence. The order must have been heard, but to my surprise the noise continued. I got to my feet and walked in the direction of the voice, crouching to avoid the bullets and stumbling over the row of outstretched legs.

I was confronted by the distraught face of a frightened glider-pilot sergeant. From it poured a stream of querulous complaint, repetitive but not hysterical, like a soldier maudlin drunk moaning on his barrack-room bed about everything and everybody. I hissed to him to shut up. The man glanced up but the babble continued. There was only one thing to do. I raised my fist and hit him full in the mouth. The noise stopped, and the man looked up at me, his face registering surprise and offence. Then I realized what I had done, but when I looked at the men sitting on either side I could see only approbation.

The shooting had now stopped, but any boat which did approach was likely to be shot out of the water. We were far too near to those Germans. So once again I dragged the men to their feet and led them downstream, walking sometimes along the narrow strip of beach, but more often wading knee deep in the water. I left the glider-pilot sergeant and the other strangers sitting there. Our own men were care enough, our close-knit unity not to be put at risk by the presence of outsiders.

After five minutes, we had covered no more than a hundred yards or so. Then, from across the water, came a new sound. It was the putter of an outboard engine; and a shape, darker even than the river, was moving towards the bank, a boat aiming towards the shore at an oblique angle. It changed direction towards us. The crew must be either bold or rash. How could they be sure that they were steering towards friends and not to a German patrol. To put their minds at rest, I hailed them and to my overwhelming relief a Canadian voice shouted back that they were coming over to pick us up.

Harrison and Williams waded out to seize the gunwale. The Canadian, calm and encouraging, was urging us to get in but not to rush, asking how many there were. They could take fourteen men. I felt the cold flatness of despair. There were fifteen of us. Someone would have to wait with me for the boat to come back for us.

The Canadians were already pulling the last men into the boat, and I was standing with Harrison alone in the river when I heard Weiner's voice harshly insisting that no one would be left behind. The young cox'n needed no further urging, but implored us to be careful as the boat was so grossly overloaded. Then Harrison pushed me up over the side, and the two of us flopped down beside the cox'n as the engine went into gear and the boat moved towards mid-stream.

Shells were dropping into the river around us. If the boat overturned, we wouldn't stand a chance. Exhausted as we were, our boots and clothing would soon drag us under water. Drowning was something new to face, and we were so very close to safety now.

Then the boat was grounding and we were tumbling over the side even more quickly than we had climbed aboard. The men pushed it off, and the cox'n circled, steering back towards the distant bank to look for another load, waving to acknowledge our chorus of fervent thanks. A shell fell near it, spouting a fountain of water into the air. The Bofors shells still streaked scarlet and streams of tracer poured across the water. I prayed that somehow those Canadians would survive the rest of the night.

It was no place to linger. Quickly we scrambled across the flat land, away from the river. Ahead a high bank loomed. I clambered up without effort, all tiredness now gone, running almost gaily down the other side. In a scurry the rest joined me. The bank shut out the battle like a curtain dropping behind us. We were safe!

A figure took shape in front of us, a military policeman of the 43rd Division, smart and dapper with his pistol and arm-band, telling us to move ahead until we found a track, which would put us on the road to Driel, about two miles away. There we would find food and transport.

As we trudged across the grass, I wondered how we would manage yet another five miles.

202

We reached the track, which after a few hundred yards led us to the road. When I stopped, the men flopped to the ground, empty and lifeless, lacking any wish to go on. More parties of men appeared through the darkness, shambling in the exhaustion of relief, all terror ended, devoid of the will-power needed to summon up further effort.

There was only one way to make the two-mile march bearable, an old fashioned remedy. I called to Sergeant Weiner to fall the men in in threes. The disciplined bark bounced back to me as Weiner pulled himself to his feet, shouting to the men to fall in. There was no trace of query or surprise in Weiner's voice, and the men shuffled to their feet.

I watched Weiner hustling them into their places, ordering them to stand still. Then I was walking down the three short ranks, looking into the faces of the fifteen men as I paused for a moment opposite each one. Everyone still carried a rifle or sub-machine-gun, either British or German, except for Williams who was still burdened with his Bren.

I told them that they would march back properly, explaining that it would be easier that way. There was agreement in their faces. Then, as if I was on a parade ground, I gave the familiar orders to close order march, turn to the right and quick march. I took my place in front; Weiner dropped to the rear. The movements were automatic. So would be this final five mile march. We stepped off down the road.

As we marched on, we met more and more remnants of the Division. Some were in small disciplined parties like our own, keeping together in single file or in bunches, but none moving in threes. There were single stragglers, groups of two or three men, some properly equipped, but many without either weapons or headgear. All were in the last stages of exhaustion, some collapsed by the roadside, incapable of going further.

Very soon we started to see signs of the 2nd Army: gun positions, the shapes of vehicles under camouflage nets, anti-tank guns covering the road, and the slit trenches of the infantry. This was the main axis of the advance, the route which the 2nd Army had found so very difficult. The long straight road across the flat dyke-scarred countryside seemed endless, but the rhythm of the men's boots striking the hard surface kept us going. Going away from the battle. But for how long? Airborne troops always found themselves back in the battle again with the infantry soon after they had been relieved. Would we be back there fighting in a week or two's time, reinforcements for some unit which had been less unlucky than ourselves?

My thoughts were interrupted by the sight of a group of buildings about a hundred yards ahead. Another red-cap motioned us towards what looked like a school, telling us that we would find food waiting inside.

I halted them. There was only the one way to end such a march. It was pointless, perhaps, but I decided to make the final gesture.

Bringing them to attention, I ordered them to slope arms, and to march by the left to attention. I sensed their appreciation as their shoulders went back. This was the way they always returned to camp. This was the way they always finished. As they stepped off for the last fifty yards, they were even swinging their arms.

I halted them outside the door. The crowd of airborne soldiers sitting or standing there turned dead and apathetic eyes towards us, murmuring their contempt for such stupidity. But I didn't care.

The crowded room was hot with the odours of cooking food and drenched clothing. We queued by a table where mugs of hot tea, laced with rum, were thrust into our hands. Men were joking and chattering all around, exhilaration

204

overcoming everything else. From another table they were being handed tin plates on to which very small helpings of stew had been ladled. I thought there must be a shortage of rations, but a subaltern who was superintending the service, contradicted my unspoken query. It was dangerous to give them a lot; the doctors were worried about the effect of too much food on empty stomachs.

Then someone ushered us outside towards a couple of jeeps. There was not room for all of us, so I sat on the bonnet of the leading one, gripping the catch to hold myself in place. After only a few yards, I started to regret my choice of seat. As I clung to the bouncing vehicle, every bump jarred my body, and the icy wind cut through my soaked clothing. The contrast to the hot room was intense. The heat drained out of me and in a few minutes I started to shiver.

Short though the ride was, the harm had been done. When the jeeps stopped, we were all ordered into a larger vehicle. One truck! Just this one truck for the Battalion! Still shivering, my numbed hands lacked the strength to pull myself over the tailboard, so that Harrison and Weiner had to hoist me in, one pulling and one pushing from behind.

The canopy of the truck now sheltered us, but my shivering became uncontrollable. I knew that I was becoming light-headed and could hear myself grieving aloud for those we had left behind, particularly for those who had been lost during the withdrawal down to the river bank.

There was silence in the truck. Then I heard, as if from a long way off, the voice of Sergeant Weiner, calm and flat, saying that none of them would have got back if it had not been for me. It was as true to say that I would never have got back if it hadn't been for them but I shall always be grateful to Weiner for having said it.

The next thing I remember was Weiner and Harrison half

carrying me into what seemed to be a hospital. Someone was stripping off my clothes and dressing me in pyjamas. Then I felt the prick of a needle in my arm.

I was awake, with the sun shining into the windows of the ward. An orderly brought tea and food on a tray. I lay between the clean sheets, looking at the torn and filthy garments on the chair by the side of the bed.

There was nothing wrong with me now. I saw that my hand was wrapped in a clean bandage. When the nursing orderly came to remove the tray, he brought the message that a soldier was waiting in the corridor to see me.

As soon as the orderly left the room, I slipped out of bed and put on my clothes. I went out into the corridor. Waiting there was Harrison, a broad smile on his face, telling me that Captain Gray and Mr Elkins had turned up with eight of the missing men. Another twenty stragglers had also arrived from somewhere or other. But that was the lot. That was the Battalion. Three officers and forty-three soldiers.

We walked together out of the door of the hospital side by side. The weak September sun shone down on the battered buildings of Nijmegen. Away in the distance the dull rumble of the battle still rolled down from the north.

THE END

POSTSCRIPT

The essence of this story is true, but after thirty years memory is fallible. The incidents which are portrayed all happened, although many of the details may be wrong. I kept no diary, and could refresh my recollections only from the official records in the Public Record Office.

The names are all imaginary, as are several of the people, particularly Harry Bates, Jimmy Gray, Robert Watson, Kelly, Bartholomew and Oswold. Some are an amalgam of personalities, half-remembered, difficult to place exactly. Many are real.

During the battle, people came and went. It was weeks and sometimes months before those of us who survived discovered what had happened to them. Our Colonel, that fine soldier and even finer man, was killed just after I left him in the woods. Of the wounded, some real and some imaginary, the Brigadier, Harry Bates, Sgt. Prior, the RSM, Private Robertson and Private Gregory were all made prisoner and survived their captivity. The story of the Brigadier's escape from hospital has often been told. The Doctor and Corporal Pritchard stayed with the wounded and were captured with them. Robert Watson, together with Douglas Thompson and CSM Huggins, were made prisoner north of Wolfhezen when that part of the Battalion which failed to cross the railway embankment was attacked and overrun during the night. Corporals Day and Galbraith, together with Lance Corporal Williams and Privates Jackson and Oswold were among those who came back across the Rhine.

This book remembers David and those others who lie in Oosterbeek Cemetery, and elsewhere.

NOTE TO THE SECOND EDITION

Leo Cooper, who first published this book, suggested to me that I should write it. The first trial chapters were not a success. To recount my personal experiences of the battle I found inhibiting. As a result we decided that I should hide my identity under a pseudonym, after which my pen moved rather more freely. Needless to say it was inevitable that my own identity and that of the unit – 156 Battalion, The Parachute Regiment – were revealed soon after publication.

The Brigadier was, of course, 'Shan' (now General Sir John) Hackett. Of the others, our Colonel was 'Dickie' (Sir Richard) des Voeux of the Grenadier Guards, his fellow Grenadier was RSM Dennis Gay, and my batman, Private Harrison, was Fred Tracey. David Unwin was Michael Page, who had been my best man, and whose son, Geoffrey, born posthumously, has produced another Michael. Luke Tyler, Weiner, Jones and John Simmonds were also real people, portrayed as well as memory served. The rest, as I said, are either imaginary or amalgams of real people.

One way or another, the writing of this book has put me in touch with many ex-members of the battalion, among others my friend Fred Tracey. Errors have been pointed out to me and this edition corrects a few. Deliberately, however, I confused the actions of 'A' and 'B' Companies during the attack on the Dreijensche Weg; this I have not changed, because, in its essence, the story is true.

Geoffrey Powell
July 1986